COUNTRY LIVING

Merry & Bright

COUNTRY LIVING

Merry & Bright

★ 301 Festive Ideas for Celebrating Christmas ★

FROM THE EDITORS OF COUNTRY LIVING

HEARST BOOKS
A division of Sterling Publishing Co., Inc

New York / London

Contents

Foreword

If you're like me, you look forward to the holiday season all year long. It's such a feast for the senses: The sight of twinkling lights, the sound of familiar carols, the smell of fresh greens, the taste of warm gingerbread, the touch of crisp gift wrap and satiny ribbon. Yet for all the anticipation, it always seems to go by too fast. Surrounded by a blur of activity, it's easy to lose sight of what matters most—coming together with family and friends and being thankful for what we have. At *Country Living*, we're always on the lookout for simple, time-saving ways to beautify your home and create meaningful memories for your family. I'm forever inspired by the homeowners, decorators, artisans, and chefs we feature every month and, of course, by our own talented staff. *Merry & Bright* is a collection of my favorite ideas for holiday decorating, baking, and crafts. Most require only an hour or an afternoon, so even the busiest among us can incorporate them into our own time-honored traditions. Whether you decide to trim your house from top to bottom or merely to add a new cookie recipe to your repertoire, hundreds of festive ideas await you on the pages ahead. From everyone at *Country Living*, I wish you a joyous Christmas!

—Nancy Mernit Soriano
Editor-in-Chief

one

Decorating

For many people the holiday season begins with opening boxes of cherished ornaments, glittery tinsel, and festive ribbons and dusting off treasured collections of holiday-themed objects. A beautiful Christmas tree is sure to be the center of attention, but decorating for the holidays also means dressing up tabletops, windowsills, banisters, fireplace mantels, and even the family piano. This is the time of year when the adage "less is more" doesn't necessarily apply. Transforming your home into a magical setting—whether simple or elaborate—is what this season is all about, along with the extra touches that help make the holidays memorable. On the following pages you'll find decorating ideas that showcase the tradition of red and green, as well as those that embrace the elegant simplicity of winter white and the romantic nature of soft pastels. Also included are tips for creating charming Christmas vignettes and for showcasing classic still lifes, as well as lots of ways to add rustic touches and numerous suggestions for using favorite collections, vintage ornaments, and beloved childhood playthings to great advantage. Whether your take on holiday decorating is traditional or modern, you're sure to find festive inspirations that are perfectly suited to your taste.

Trim the tree in its holiday best with these ideas ranging from timeless tradition to pure fantasy.

①

2. Be sure to vary the size, scale, and shapes of ornaments as you apply them. Oversize balls immediately add lots of color and also light up darker areas of the tree. Start with the largest ornaments and layer them evenly throughout, then work toward the smaller ones. Cluster ornaments together (odd numbers work best) for even greater impact.

3. Reinvent your tree with gifts from the sea. Seashells, dried starfish, and sand dollars embellish this enormous tree.

1. Trim your tree with golden treasures. Glass balls, vintage bead garlands, and keepsakes from the attic adorn a tree made all the more striking by a gold tone-on-tone palette.

4. String garlands of popcorn and cranberries for rustic simplicity. Apples and pears are tied to branches with red ribbon glued to their stems. Dried orange slices mimic stained glass when the sun shines through them, adding a subtle sparkle to the tree. A tin bucket holds the tree.

5. Use a champagne bucket as a one-of-a-kind tree stand for a small tree or tree top. This conifer top (often sold by tree farms and vendors) sits in a sterling silver champagne bucket, and is decorated with vivid robin's egg blue ornaments, small faux birds' nests, and handmade taffeta birds.

④

⑤

6. Decorate your tree entirely with handmade ornaments crafted by local artisans. This tree is adorned with cherubs made from beeswax, stars and snowflakes made out of tin, snowflakes and garlands woven with wheat, hand-painted wooden Santas, and translucent hand-blown glass balls.

7. All it took to decorate this tree was a few natural touches: a flock of merry cardinals, a pinecone garland, and a sage-colored sash of satin ribbon.

8. Hang a charming doll's skate on the tree.

9. Use ribbons in jewel-tone colors and wispy lengths to decorate a small tree. This is a fast, easy, and romantic way to trim a tree.

10. Before you decorate an artificial tree, be sure to fluff it. An hour or two before you begin, take the tree parts out of its box or storage bag. The stand holds the trunk pieces, which stack on top of each other. Slip the branches into place (there are holes or hinges in the trunk), stroking the needles to puff them up. For a more realistic trunk, bend the branches so they look more natural (optional).

decorating

12. Why not place a second tree in the family room or kitchen? A small tree evokes the Christmas spirit without getting in the way. Full- and child-size utensils decorate this tree, along with homespun touches, such as a popcorn garland and crisp gingham ribbons.

11. Play on the end-of-year aspect of Father Time with a collection of vintage clock faces. With their bold graphics, nostalgic charm, and center holes for hanging, old clock faces make inspired ornaments. String them onto the tree with ribbon. The tree topper is fashioned from photocopies of clock faces outlined in gold tinsel and attached with wire (like exploding clock springs) to a glittery gold star. The vibrant pink-and-gold color scheme extends to Christmas stockings and a tree skirt fashioned from old quilts.

13. Festoon your tree with ornaments that complement your home's décor. The silvered pinecones, garlands, beads, bells, birds, and balls with modest touches of blue pick up the room's color scheme. A crescent-shaped French table makes a fashionable tree stand.

14. Adorn the tree with inspirational words. Fabric trim, beaded snowflakes, and inspirational words hand-stamped onto pink-sheared parchment paper echo the holiday theme.

15. Everyone has his own preference for a fresh tree: For hanging ornaments, the sturdiest branches belong to the blue spruce. Firs are the most fragrant and long lasting. Scotch pines hold their needles even when dry.

16. Vintage letters culled from old signs, printers' type, and alphabet teaching aids festoon this tree. The letters are arranged to spell out holiday words, such as "ho ho ho" and "holly." The red and green color scheme emphatically says "Christmas."

17. 'Tis the tartan season! Dress the tree in a tartan garland and ribbons.

18. Inspired by a love of French country antiques, this tree was decorated with silk sunflowers, hydrangeas, peonies, roses, and ribbons.

19. What will you use as a tree topper? Consider the unexpected: a cluster of ornaments or a single oversize piece related to your theme.

17

19

20. Create a tree-trimming toolbox. Keep these and all your other tree-trimming essentials (see list below) in a small toolbox to ensure the decorating process goes off without a hitch.

- *wire cutters*
- *glue*
- *scissors*
- *ornament hooks*
- *nylon fishing line*
- *paper clips*
- *thin ribbon*
- *invisible tape*

21. For a mix of rustic charm and casual chic, festoon your tree with feathers, a bird's nest, and mercury glass balls. A galvanized bucket frosted with snow holds this spindly tree upright.

22. Use your collections to create one-of-a-kind decorations. Leather-buttoned baby shoes capture the innocence of the season, while three little handmade bears relax near a holiday fir anchored in a Bennington stoneware crock.

25

26. Choose a tree that is slightly too tall for the room in which it will be displayed. Once you get the tree home, trim off the spindly top branches so it fits, which also makes the tree look fuller.

23. Decorative gift tags can be called into service as ornaments. Dove-shaped gift tags are the perfect lightweight ornaments for a reproduction feather tree set in a galvanized paint bucket.

24. Top your tree with a feathered friend. This tinsel tree is festooned with glass birds, red-beaded tassels, and clear crystals topped with a bird made from red fabric.

25. Celebrate simply. This Douglas fir looks grand adorned exclusively with cut-paper snowflakes. Galvanized geese take on a fanciful air with red ribbon tied around their necks.

★ decorating

26

27. A simple Christmas starts with pure white. Enhance an unpruned tree with tiny white lights; here, two white teddy bears evoke the charm and innocence of the holiday.

28. Go faux! They look natural—well, some of them do—and they save time. This lifelike Douglas fir is bedecked with a striking gold and teal color scheme with a string of lights sheathed in gold ribbon.

29. To water the tree easily, use an automotive funnel with a long, flexible neck. Rest the funnel's tip in the stand, and use a measuring cup to pour water through. Cover the tree skirt with a towel to protect it from drips.

30. Give your tree a romantic flair with pastel-colored ornaments. Fan ornaments, flowers, candles, and a blown-glass garland evoking candies adorn the deep green tree.

31. Use antique ornaments and trinkets discovered at flea markets and garage sales to dress up your tree. Underneath the tree are vintage trunks découpaged with reproduction wrapping paper.

32. Why not opt for a themed tree? Here are a few ideas:

- *an angel tree*
- *a snowflake tree*
- *a "seasonal" tree reflecting the seasons of the year*
- *a New Year's tree decorated with champagne bottles, champagne glasses, top hats, mirror balls, stars, streamers, noisemakers, and party favors*
- *a state tree decorated with the state bird and flower as well as other state symbols*
- *a "musical" tree decorated with glowing musical instruments*

34. Go vintage from top to bottom. This all-white tree brings back memories of the post-World War Two era with its over-size tree lights and hand-blown ornaments.

33. Use unexpected colors and patterns to create some Christmas magic. A cocoa-colored pom-pom garland, woven birch-and-rattan spheres, peacock-plumed partridges fashioned from an old patchwork skirt, tartan bows, and flocked-glass balls in warm hues of chocolate and gold offer a pleasing alternative to traditional holiday reds and greens.

35. To achieve an old-fashioned look, drape your tree with vintage blown-glass garlands. If you find incomplete strands at flea markets, string several strands together to create a complete garland.

decorating

★

(36)

36. Decorate your tree exclusively with ribbons. Vintage plaid and striped ribbons are tied into loose bows on this Douglas fir.

37. Tree toppers come in a variety of shapes and can capture the mood of the moment: the season's hope with a star, its divinity with an angel, and its simplicity with an elegant spire.

(37)

38. In a sweet twist on candy canes dangling from the holiday tree, iced cookies are hooked onto the boughs of the sturdy-branched fir—no strings attached. (To make a batch of edible ornaments, try our Candy Cane cookie recipe on page 184.) Tartan ribbon serves as the Christmas tree garland.

40. Decorate your tree entirely with red amaryllis blooms. It requires a little effort, but the effect is memorable. A smattering of silver ornaments and a string of twinkling lights cast a glow on the red blossoms.

41. Give your tree the royal treatment. This dazzling eleven-foot Fraser fir is laden with hundreds of vintage ornaments. Oversize pinecones, elegantly beribboned gifts, white amaryllis, and a simple fir garland and wreath, hanging on a weathered barn door, complete the festive effect.

39. There are no rules when it comes to holiday decorating: Bring unexpected things to unexpected places. With tiny golden lights tucked inside and around them, nineteenth-century apothecary and remedy bottles make this kitchen's evergreen glisten.

41

42. Decorate your tree with cherished child-hood mementos. Animal crackers, stuffed animals, and quirky figurines are hung on this "toy" tree.

43. To give your tree an Early-American feel, choose white lights, natural materials, and hand-made ornaments.

44. Use paper dolls to decorate the tree. These work best on trees where there is plenty of space between each branch.

45. To strike a balance between bare branches and ornament overload, use the following guidelines. As a rule, use one set of 50 lights per foot of tree.

Tree Height	Number of Bulbs	Number of Decorations
2 feet	100–150	25–35
3 feet	150–250	35–50
4 feet	200–350	50–75
6 feet	300–450	100–150
7 feet	350–550	150–200

Add holiday **sparkle** to any room
with these **ornament ideas**.

46. Before mixing new and vintage ornaments on a tree, set the new ones in a glass bowl on a windowsill for a few months so the sunlight has a chance to soften their colors.

47. Lose your original ornament storage box? Simple cardboard egg cartons offer an orderly way to safeguard ornaments from one season to the next.

48. Use slightly damaged vintage ornaments, such as birds in a tinsel nest that lack the part that clips it to a branch, in tabletop displays.

(49)

(50)

(51)

49. Hang an ornament on a festive ribbon from the top of a hutch or shelves.

50. Use ornaments to create festive accents all around your house: the front hallway, a stairway landing, a neglected corner or side table. Here, vintage glass ornaments in an English ironstone basin anchor a collection of unmatched silver candlesticks.

51. Embellish a curtain tieback with shimmering ornaments.

54. Handcraft tree ornaments from manila gift tags decorated with rubber stamps or photographs of family and friends.

52. To show off a collection of vintage glass balls or other ornaments, place them in paper candy and cupcake cups and display on a favorite plate.

53. Age ornaments by exposing them to the elements. These ornaments achieved their pearly patina after sitting in a garden for six months where they served as miniature gazing globes. The unpolished champagne bucket boasts a mottled tarnish that perfectly complements the cool luster of the ornaments.

★ decorating

41

55. Keep an eye out for inexpensive single ornaments, incomplete boxed sets, or balls exhibiting wear and tear whenever you peruse the aisles of a flea market or the booths of an antiques mall. Items that are too worn to hang on a tree can be piled in a pretty bowl, arranged in an apothecary jar, or nestled among the greenery on a mantel.

57

56. Even childhood playthings can be incorporated into your holiday décor. In an antique English transferware compote, a lovingly worn teddy bear embraces a vintage ornament, exuding the sweetness of the season.

57. Make little touches as much a part of the holidays as elaborate ones. Charm guests in the powder room with a tarnished compote brimming with pearly baubles, a subtle bow to the season.

58. Create a delicate still life by pairing an heirloom ornament with a baby shoe, evoking a wistful nostalgia for times gone by.

58

decorating

★

43

(59)

(60)

59. Group holiday ornaments and other treasures in your prettiest bowls and pots. Here, in a sturdy English ironstone bowl, simple silver and gold balls are clustered in a nest of yard-sale tinsel.

60. A single special ornament can be elevated to a striking focal point when set apart under glass or on a pedestal. Here, a hand-painted ornament rests atop a McCoy cornucopia vase.

61. For a display that sparkles, fill a milk-glass compote with a collection of vintage glass ornaments.

(61)

63. Proper storage will preserve the condition of your ornaments for years to come. The ideal storage container is a rigid box with compartments or adjustable dividers to prevent delicate pieces from knocking against each other. For added protection, wrap each ornament in acid-free tissue, acid-free paper towels, or 100 percent cotton. Never wrap ornaments in plastic, bubble wrap, or newspaper. Finally, a closet in the main living area of the house is the idea location for storing boxes of ornaments. Attics and garages suffer from temperature fluctuations, and basements tend to be damp or prone to flooding. If you must use the basement, place the boxes on a high shelf with the heaviest box on the bottom of the stack.

62. Silver and gold make the holidays sparkle. Coil a small silver tinsel garland into a pedestal for a pretty gold ornament.

decorating

★

45

Offer a **warm** welcome to holiday guests with any one of these **stylish wreaths**.

66. To extend the welcome at your front door, lasso a large wreath to a small one with a slip knot; tie both ends at the top in a big bow.

64. Use a wreath to dress up furniture, such as this armoire. This lovely lush wreath is composed of artificial branches that were filled in with real leaves fastened with wire, then adorned with a few personal touches and finished with a satin bow.

65. Accent the season with the scent of fresh herbs. This "culinary" wreath is made from bunches of sage, oregano, rosemary, and bay leaves.

67. For a seaside theme, embellish a wreath with starfish and sea urchins.

68. Christmas in the country lends itself to creative touches of rustic charm. This handmade cedar wreath is decorated with clusters of pepperberry and hydrangea heads, pinecones, pheasant feathers, and a tiny nest of eggs (here filled with robin's egg soaps) and an extravagant organza bow.

69

69. Use roses in your holiday wreath. This tight circle of blossoms is set atop a wreath of moss-covered twigs and rose hips.

70. Use multiple wreaths to decorate shelves and punctuate with jewel-toned ornaments or other trinkets.

70

71. Embellish a plain wreath with treasures from the outdoors: A diminutive bird's nest, pinecones, feathers, and berries are accented with a red-and-white gingham bow.

72. Instead of ornaments, decorate a wreath with apples.

73. Accessorize a wreath with a favorite treasure, which in this case is a beloved pair of time-worn ice skates.

74. Transform a fifty-cent yard-sale find like this macaroni wreath into a holiday treasure with metallic spray paint.

75. Tuck holiday cards into a silver metal wreath of leaves and flowers.

76. Festoon the front door with a fragrant wreath fashioned from fresh pine, cedar, hydrangea, and green apples.

Decorate every corner of the house with all that delights you.

78

77. Use a favorite cup (this one is pink luster-ware) and a handful of small pinecones to show-case a diminutive bottle-brush tree.

78. For an elegantly rustic look, trim the man-tel with a simple garland of evergreen and berries and a row of stockings made with vintage fabrics.

decorating

★

55

79. Use a white palette for a sense of serenity. Pillar candles, pearl buttons, and a wrought-iron mirror lend a romantic feel to the mantel.

80. Transform the mantel into a festive stage by pairing vintage ornaments with a collection of vintage bottles. Green and gold French and German hand-painted ornaments (including some in a rare teardrop shape) resemble jeweled stoppers perched atop early twentieth-century glass bottles.

79

80

81. Stage a charming holiday farm scene on the mantel with a herd of antique German sheep and a lighted cabin.

82. Embellish a mantel with a silvery wreath from the craft store and diminutive gift boxes.

83. A mixture of indoor and outdoor items makes for a refreshingly unconventional mantel arrangement.

84. Mount a trio of lemon-leaf wreaths around a gilt-framed mirror.

85. Candles are one of the most conspicuous fire threats, no matter the time of year. Never leave lit candles unattended: do not use them on trees or other greenery, and keep them well clear of any kind of paper. Holders must be nonflammable and stable, so candles can't be knocked down or blown over.

86. The beauty of pinecones makes them an ideal decoration during the holidays. Here, a garland made out of pinecones frames a fireplace, and pinecones in urns grace the mantel.

87. Placing objects under glass automatically creates intrigue. Here, a small tree and a miniature ice-skater are showcased under a cloche, making a charming holiday vignette.

88. Ribbons dress things up, whether they're the finishing touch on a wrapped gift or simply tied around a terra-cotta pot (or cloth dinner napkin). Transform a bowl of pretty pears perched on a bed of boxwood into a lovely centerpiece by tying velvet bows onto their stems.

89. Hang bird-shaped ornaments around a birdhouse, creating a festive outdoor scene.

90. Fragrance is as much a part of holiday décor as trees and ornaments. Here, a small tree made of boxwood sprigs stuck in damp florist's foam is decorated with orange-clove pomanders and a garland of dried rose hips.

91. Use ribbon to hang a collection of ornaments in a window. Here, we've used sky blue organza.

92. Festoon a banister with cedar, bay, and eucalyptus greenery along with silvery beads.

93. Prop vintage postcards in antique florists' frogs.

94. Arrange bunches of fresh herbs, lavender, dried orange slices, and soft clumps of moss on a serving platter to fill your home with the aroma of a holiday potpourri.

(94)

96. No room left on the mantel? You can always find another spot to display your holiday collections. Here a contingent of Santas, made of all manner of materials and each with his own name, convenes on a kitchen table, where some are supported by picnic hampers covered in scarlet tartan. Above them hangs a wreath, to which a quirky selection of found objects were glued.

97. To establish a festive air, all it takes are a few touches of red and green deftly applied throughout the house. The key to this classic approach is to be consistent with both your palette and your materials.

95. To dress your bed with a magical holiday touch, drape garlands of glass beads through the bed frame and use gingham ribbon to suspend wreaths of paperwhites. They will scent the room for about a week.

98. Create a holiday display inside a cabinet or cupboard by replacing everyday items with angels and apples.

99. Never burn candles for more than a couple of hours at a time. Be safe: pin a wide ribbon around the candle's base, and extinguish the flame before the candle burns down to that point.

(98)

(99)

(102) **102.** Single out a few perfect roses from a bouquet. Knot lengths of rich satin ribbon around the lower stems and suspend them from the top of a cabinet door. Save the ribbons and use to hang favorite ornaments or a fresh group of roses next year.

100. Look around your home for unusual display pieces. This pair of ironstone gravy boats makes perfect planters. To brighten the display, consider using silver. By placing the gravy boats on a silver platter, each element of the composition is accentuated.

101. For a different take on Christmas red, use magenta and fuchsia as your main colors and supplement them with bright reds, silvers, and even rich blues. The combination maintains the red theme even though other colors are used.

(103)

106. Only purchase lights that are UL-approved. Before using, thoroughly check both the new and old sets for damaged sockets, frayed wires, burned-out bulbs, and faulty connections. Never decorate metal trees with electric lights. Turn off all the lights, indoors and out, if you leave the house or go to sleep.

103. Make the most of every piece: Stacking several antique silver compotes allows for a much more dramatic display.

104. Decorate a doorknob with a papier-mâché cone filled with silk flowers.

105. Looking to add some dazzle to your home this holiday season? Gold, in all its luster, offers a brilliant alternative to traditional garnet and green. The wreath and garland around this fireplace are studded with red berries and gold ornaments and dappled with gold paint, while old-fashioned feather trees decorated with gold ornaments brighten the hearth.

(104)

107. A simple combination of greenery, white pots, and a grouping of pinecones makes an elegant holiday decoration.

108. In a clear glass vase, cranberries make an excellent base for an arrangement of blooms.

109. Keep your holiday decorations fresh. In many homes, holiday displays appear the day after Thanksgiving and remain up through Epiphany or longer. Renew the look from time to time by adding fresh-cut greens from the garden (they are both festive and free).

(108)

(110)

110. Make your collections come alive by displaying them in unexpected ways. A collection of colored-glass balls in canning jars can be placed anywhere a touch of color is needed.

111. Let your imagination take wing. Here, bare branches covered in gold glitter provide a sculptural perch for Victorian-style glass birds, paper birdhouses (see page 162 for how-to), and a cascade of birch leaves in parchment.

114. In lieu of a wreath, hang a basket filled with greenery and a charming Santa figure on the door.

112. With a fine ribbon, even a humble pinecone becomes a masterpiece. Venture out-doors and look around. The tiniest twig, a simple pinecone, or a smidgen of greenery sings when turned into a focal point.

113. Incorporate a pineapple into your holiday décor. Pineapples are Early American symbols of welcome.

117. For a fresh take on displaying your holiday wreath this season, highlight it in a picture frame: Measure a length of thick ribbon so when suspended, the wreath hangs centered in the frame. Wrap the ribbon around the top of the wreath and tie it to the top of the frame, creating a bow at the top. Hang the frame on a wall hook.

118. Showcase your collections. In this photo, brush trees from the 1950s, made from bottle-cleaning brushes, parade across a shelf along with a row of glowing votives.

115. Whether crimson, scarlet, or burgundy, red captures the eye. In a white hallway, a wire urn filled with shiny red ornaments becomes an instant focal point.

116. Cinnamon is a classic holiday scent. Tie ribbons around a small bunch of cinnamon sticks and set them near a warm fire to fill the room with warm, spicy fragrance.

119

122. Dressing up the banister is a great way to add holiday charm to a staircase. But don't forget the stairs themselves. If they're wide enough, place a poinsettia, a small wrapped gift, or a vintage children's toy on the side of each step.

119. A banister offers ample opportunity for holiday adornment. Use satin ribbons, strings of beads, and garlands of greenery.

120. Embellish your chandelier with moss, twigs, and icy crystal beads.

121. Repetition is often the key to interesting decorating. Here, the circle is repeated, and the red-and-white theme reinforced, in a collection of new and vintage wreaths and an ironstone plate.

120

(123)

125. Use a bench on the front porch to create a still life. Arrange a bed of greenery on the seat, nestle pinecones into the greenery, and tuck colorful ornaments among the pinecones to create a welcoming wintery scene.

123. Use a coffee cup to serve up a seasonal display.

124. Drape a bed frame with an evergreen garland hung with silver pinecone ornaments.

(124)

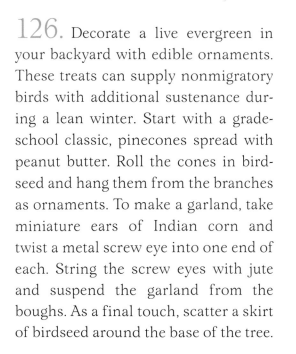

126. Decorate a live evergreen in your backyard with edible ornaments. These treats can supply nonmigratory birds with additional sustenance during a lean winter. Start with a grade-school classic, pinecones spread with peanut butter. Roll the cones in bird-seed and hang them from the branches as ornaments. To make a garland, take miniature ears of Indian corn and twist a metal screw eye into one end of each. String the screw eyes with jute and suspend the garland from the boughs. As a final touch, scatter a skirt of birdseed around the base of the tree.

127. Transform humble objects into artful curiosities by placing them in or under glass. Here, a mix of old and new ornaments shimmer like jewels.

★

decorating

83

128. Why should a love of roses be confined to a single season? Roses can add timeless charm to all sorts of holiday decorating schemes. Remnants of floral fabric and trim are easily transformed into unique Christmas stockings; embellish them with pearl buttons.

129. A soothing palette of white is enhanced by touches of green. Here, a simple boxwood wreath adorns a cupboard door while a white ironstone bowl filled with seashells rests on a bed of greenery.

130. Perch a small toy on the treetop instead of an angel. (Secure it with thin wire.)

131. A perfectly placed decoration speaks volumes. Red-and-white stockings hung against a white background add a touch of whimsy to the holiday season.

132. Place vases and urns filled with greenery throughout the house. This iron urn holds juniper, cedar, and balsam branches. A felt Santa hangs above.

(133)

133. Add a flourish to a stairway's newel post.

134. Wind a garland up a banister or hang it in swags along a fireplace mantel. Wire together real fruit, such as limes, small apples, pears, and lemons (they'll last for about two weeks), secure them at intervals along the garland, and finish with lustrous satin ribbon.

135. Gather your unmatched porcelain teacups and place tea lights (in their own plastic or metal holders) inside. The thin porcelain will glow from the light of the flame.

136. Fit one vase inside a larger vase of the same shape so that fresh flowers and shiny ornaments can coexist.

137. Showcase your tree toppers by placing them on sconces. Remove the bulb casing or candle and slip the tree topper onto the base (you may need to use some tacking gum to help keep it in place). The reflective quality of the parabolic sconce, like the one shown here, will enhance the color or shimmery effect of the tree topper.

138. Embellish an all-white garland with old-fashioned paper dolls and drape it around the window.

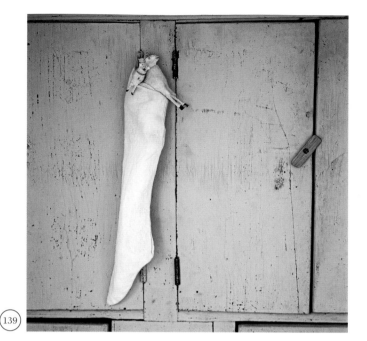

141. Use children's toys to decorate a windowsill, the fireplace mantel, under the tree, or anywhere that could use a spot of holiday cheer. An antique fire engine, a teddy bear, or beloved doll can add a touch of nostalgia to any nook or cranny.

139. Tuck a pair of wee animals—stuffed teddy bears, small dogs, or a rabbit or two—into a stocking and hang from a doorknob, mantel, or other prominent spot.

140. For a charming centerpiece or tabletop decoration, cluster a group of diminutive animal figurines on a white plate or serving platter. Place an ornament in the center.

142. It's not always necessary to alter rooms theatrically for the holidays. For a more subtle nod to the season, choose a few spots to make a unique statement. Here, a flock of old straw goats, bound with red cotton strips, stand together at the base of a door.

143. When time is at a premium, uncomplicated displays are best. Here, an old transferware tureen, without its lid, makes a good container for vintage books and holiday sweets.

(143)

(144)

144. The color white adapts beautifully to any season. In winter it lends a splendid purity and innocence to the holiday, conjuring up notions of snow, sweet frosting, and angels. Stockings fashioned from old white textiles keep the focus on the holiday.

145. Look to the garden for fresh ideas for every corner of the house. Here, evergreen boughs and red roses crown a portrait; a *Eugenia* standard topiary is a good alternative to a table-top Christmas tree; the floral swags on its terra-cotta pot echo the carvings on the half-moon table on which it stands. A cast-iron trough holds a trio of potted boxwood plants.

146. Don't overlook the most humble of spots—hang hand-knit stockings from the knob of the bedroom closet.

147. Create a nostalgic farm vignette around the base of a small tree. Here, two charming scenes surround this tabletop tree, one on the table and one on the floor.

(146)

(147)

148. When it's time to decorate your rooms for the holidays, it's best to follow your own instincts, not the latest trends. If your heart belongs to shiny tinsel and colored lights, by all means use them to make your season merry.

149. A quartet of beeswax candles in the shape of pinecones makes a pretty tabletop or mantel decoration. Scatter pine needles around the base for added effect.

(149)

150. Use children's toys to create an enchanting holiday display. Here, a Victorian child's wooden wagon holds a handcrafted teddy bear and reproductions of a folk art china doll and dollhouse.

(151)

(150)

151. Merge collections to create a surprising view that delights the eye. A collection of seashells mixed with silvery mercury-glass ornaments in an ironstone bowl yields a simple yet intriguing combination of shapes.

152. Some pieces of furniture are ideal for decorating. A piano stands in for a mantel as the perfect place to hang stockings and top with a collection of birdhouses and greenery.

153. For a finishing touch to your banister decorations, prop a teddy bear with a sleigh bell on the newel post.

154. Extend a holiday theme into other rooms of the house. All it takes is a simple wreath and a few garlands of greenery to imbue a room with holiday spirit.

155. The best material for stringing garlands of popcorn, gumdrops, or cranberries is waxed tooth floss. It's strong and slick, so the items slide on easily.

156. Gather a collection of dazzling baubles in a serving platter to create a sparkling stage for a tabletop tree. Here, a small statue of Our Lady of Grace presides over a collection of silver, gold, and blue ornaments in a vintage platter set atop a silver tray.

157. Festoon the chandelier. Like a crowning jewel, this chandelier is draped in a strand of metallic beads and decorated with ornaments and fresh blooms.

159. Pair fresh-cut flowers in a single unexpected color—pink, for example—with antique silver and mercury glass for an elegant presentation.

160. Hang holiday stockings throughout the house. Stockings in the unexpected palette of pink and yellow are suspended from the banister with stockings in the more traditional colors of white and red.

161. Create a quick-and-easy holiday decoration by spray painting pinecones white and gathering them in a white bowl or serving platter.

(160)

158. Incorporating faux or dried elements into your arrangements is a great way to save on the cost of seasonal decorating. And mixing the two together makes it almost impossible to tell which are the replicas.

(161)

162. Revisit holidays gone by with ornaments and baubles from decades past. Wallpaper from the 1940s provides a nostalgic backdrop upon which glass balls, crystal candlesticks, and gold-rimmed platters sparkle. Antique Christmas cards artistically grace the mantel. Trinkets rest inside stockings fabricated from salvaged woolens and personalized with appliqués, old beads, and buttons.

163. Look for unusual places to embellish with holiday greenery. Here, berry branches crown a bucolic nineteenth-century scene.

164. A palette of red and green fills a home with holiday spirit. Plaids and toiles in classic red and green upholster the furniture, accented by the gifts wrapped in red and green paper. Apples and pears on the tree celebrate a year of bountiful blessings, a simple wreath hangs above the fieldstone fireplace, and a pair of plain woolen socks that is hung by the chimney honors the spirit of simplicity.

two

Entertaining and Tabletop Decorating

One of the greatest joys of the holidays is spending time with family and friends. Sitting around a fireplace, hosting parties, or gathering around the table to savor a special meal, share stories, and revel in the welcoming atmosphere is what the season is all about. Whether you're offering a light afternoon buffet or a six-course extravaganza, set the scene by transforming your table into a shimmering tableau by using your best china, most beautiful crystal, and favorite silver. Grace the table with your most luxurious table linens and set the mood by putting out lots of glowing candles. Create an enchanting centerpiece and accessorize each place setting with a festive place card and seasonal napkin rings. An artful arrangement of mix-and-match tableware reflects a casual chic feel, while using heirloom china and crystal sets a rich, elegant tone. Cherished collections can be used as centerpieces, either on their own or adorned with ribbons and other festive embellishments. And why not bring the outdoors in by using greenery, either as part of a centerpiece or as a way to embellish place cards? A trio of candles encircled with wisps of greenery makes a simple, elegant centerpiece, but for those who believe that "more is more," don't hesitate to create an elaborate tabletop scene. After all, this is the time of year to gather 'round to eat, drink, and be merry!

Make **merry** with family and friends around a beautiful **holiday table**.

167. Dress the dining table in variations of white: Here, a white McCoy vase filled with snow-white clusters of narcissus, white candlesticks, lace-edged linens, and transfer-decorated china combine to make an elegant and sophisticated holiday table.

165. Tagged with guests' names and placed in ironstone butter pats, small ornaments can serve as place cards on the holiday table (and afterwards, can go home with the guests as party favors). Name tags can be taped to individual dishes, as here, or attached directly to ornament hooks.

166. For a dessert buffet, vary the heights of serving pieces, using pedestal cake stands, either alone or stacked to create tiers.

entertaining and tabletop decorating

★

(168)

(170)

170. Buffets deserve attention, too. Greenery, a white candelabra, a wreath composed of jingle bells, and twig trees add sparkle and whimsy to this sideboard.

168. Pewter chargers (these are Early American reproductions) add an old-fashioned feel to the holiday table. The dinner napkin is simply tied with a red ribbon and a sprig of greenery.

169. Hand tie bows onto glasses so guests can easily identify which is theirs.

(169)

172. The busy holiday season gives us countless reasons to gather together with family and friends. Invite guests to stop by your home after a school concert, ice skating, or Christmas dinner for a sweet finale of desserts and refreshments.

173. For an elegant presentation on your buffet table, use a cake stand. Silver dragées provide a sophisticated touch, while the quiet shimmer of glass and candlelight gives this table its classic simplicity.

171. Place-card holders good enough to eat may not last the meal. Here, chocolate snowflake cookies (recipe, page 175) with dainty touches of icing suggest the delicious fare ahead. Use a family heirloom recipe or make a few extras of your favorites. Large cookies are less likely to break— or disappear—before dessert.

entertaining and tabletop decorating

★

175. Personalize a place setting by using a gold glitter pen to monogram an ornament, napkin, or place card.

176. Add a golden touch to your place settings. White china rimmed with gold stands out against gold chargers while jingle bells add a festive note to each guest's plate. Tiny pinecones accented with gold serve as place-card holders.

174. Delight guests by laying a holiday table that is brought to life by the magic of gold. The neutral backdrop, provided by a linen tablecloth topped with a wool runner, and the wool and cashmere throws, shimmers when punctuated with touches of gold. You can never use too much gold, as long as you start with a neutral base or a crisp, white tablecloth or runner. From there, layer on the gold with chargers, dishes, flatware, or crystal.

(177)

179. Use cupcake or candy paper cups to hold jelly beans in varying shades of white and other neutrals.

177. Arrange citrus fruits, pinecones, and greenery on small plates that can be removed quickly and easily at mealtime.

178. Infuse your holiday gathering with nostalgia by collecting vintage ornaments and figurines. Chenille tabletop trees and a candy-coated color scheme bring this dining room to life.

(179)

★

entertaining and tabletop decorating

180. There are myriad ways to infuse your holiday place settings with accents from the outdoors. A crimson Lady apple (from the grocery store) gains luster when given a dusting of glitter and creatively embellished with a small red bird.

(180)

181. For the table, a graceful footed candy dish or compote made from pewter or blown glass is the ideal presentation for old-fashioned ribbon candy. A tower of small fruits, such as clementines or Lady apples, would also make a lovely display. Embellish the arrangement with sprigs of evergreen and place in an easy-to-reach spot.

182. Use individual pastry tins as candleholders for glitter-dusted votives.

(182)

★

183. Attach a name tag to a Victorian Christmas light for a personalized place card at your holiday dinner.

184. Stir anticipation by using oversized invitations to announce your party.

185. Buy petits fours from a local bakery and decorate them with a holiday theme.

★

186. Bring the frosty elegance of the winter world indoors with your table settings. In a table setting evocative of the bright seasonal land-scape, snowy whites and earthy browns team up with sky blues and winterberry reds. A white cotton cloth covers the table, creating a pris-tine base for bottle-brush trees, pinecone place-card holders, and tableware bearing naturalistic motifs. Bell jars borrowed from the garden sparkle.

187. White on white can be magical. Here, three white pedestal stands are stacked one atop the other and crowned with a charming white snow figure.

Treasures **old** and **new** share the tabletop spotlight.

188. Use a row of glass vases filled with red roses for centerpieces. Shimmering glass dominates this simple but elegantly dressed table.

189. Use a pair of berry-studded topiaries in antique urns as centerpieces on a buffet table.

190. Gather an assortment of Victorian Christmas lights in a compote or on a cake stand for a festive holiday centerpiece.

191. To make an elegant holiday centerpiece, fill a glass compote with miniature Christmas balls, then nestle the stems of fresh-cut rosebuds in among the ornaments to hold them in place.

193. Create a tasty centerpiece for your dining table or buffet: Stack a graduated trio of footed glass compotes. Secure each pedestal to the next larger one with florist's putty, and fill the bowls with festive candies.

(193)

192. A new tinsel tree and pearlescent ornaments make a gleaming centerpiece on an old pine dining table.

194. You can always depend on candles to create captivating and inexpensive focal points on your holiday table.

★

Enchanting ideas for wrapping party favors.

195. Tuck party favors or small gifts inside paper cones, each with its own handcrafted gift tag attached, and gather together in a large white basket.

196. Prepare goody bags for guests to take home after a party. These bags are fashioned from vintage white linens and filled with iced gingerbread men and other holiday cookies.

197. Beautifully wrapped presents make pretty party favors. Inside the box guests might find the perfect chocolate, an elegant soap, or a shimmering ornament.

 (196)

(197)

entertaining and tabletop decorating

★

123

198. Dish out diminutive party favors from an elegant serving vessel, such as this compote of textured milk glass. Tiny scalloped name tags hang on silver elastic strings.

199. Fill take-out containers with nests of tissue paper or raffia and tuck treats—chocolates, an ornament, or a little toy—inside. Secure each box with a colorful ribbon and stack on a cake stand until guests depart.

entertaining and tabletop decorating

★

125

three

Crafts

There is nothing like a handmade decoration to show friends and loved ones how much you care. Homemade trimmings are often cherished the most, as they hold the dearest memories, but you needn't be an expert crafter to make a special gift or holiday decoration. To craft a card, stocking, or wreath or to add a touch of whimsy—or elegance—to a wrapped package, all that's required is a little time, a little effort, and a little imagination. Simple green wreaths can be transformed into one-of-a-kind pieces by attaching ribbons, flowers, birds' nests, or childhood keepsakes, such as baby shoes. Christmas cards from years past can be turned into gift tags or wreaths, while vintage cashmere sweaters can be transformed into stockings to be hung from a mantel or the backs of chairs. Colorful ribbons, old buttons, or something from the outdoors, such as a wisp of greenery or a cluster of small pinecones, are easy ways to add a personal touch to wrapped presents. On the pages that follow, you will find fabulous ideas for gift wrapping, wreath-making, and ornament crafting that range from rustic to simple to sophisticated and that reflect the magic of this joyful season.

Transform humble objects into
memorable wreaths.

201

202. As an alternative to a traditional wreath, make a cascade wreath of sugar-frosted artificial fruit. Sugar-frost artificial fruit with glitter after spray painting them white, then pin the clusters of fruit to an inverted narrow triangle of Styrofoam. To make the clusters, pierce the bottom of each piece of fruit with a florist's pin and wrap the pin with wire, twisting several wires together. As a finishing touch, use a hot glue gun to stud the cascade with kiwi-colored glass ornaments. Tie a bow of sheer and gingham ribbons at the top to add color.

200. Instead of a traditional holiday wreath on the front door, try a silvery cone of jingle bells embellished with a beautifully tied bow. Working from the bottom up, use florists' pins to fasten bells to an inverted triangle of Styrofoam. Tie on a bow fashioned from extra-wide ribbon.

201. If your collection of ornaments has grown beyond what your Christmas tree can accommodate, create a wreath: use a hot glue gun to secure ornaments of all sizes and colors to a polystyrene wreath form (available at craft stores), then hang with a ribbon.

(203)

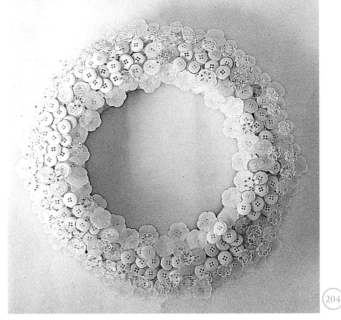

(204)

204. Dip into your button collection and make an all-white button wreath. All you need is a wreath form, buttons, and a hot glue gun.

205. Make a wreath with humble objects found around the house. Here, tin cans, chipped terra-cotta pots, and an array of conifer cones and greenery mingle surprisingly well.

203. Make a pinwheel wreath out of the funny papers. To make a pinwheel, take a newspaper square and beginning at each corner, make a cut toward the center of the square (but not all the way through), forming four triangles. Bring one corner of each triangle to the center of the square and secure with paper glue. Repeat to make more pinwheels. Adhere the finished pinwheels to a round Styrofoam wreath base.

(205)

206. Hang a wreath within a wreath for added dimension. To make, you'll need:

- *tallow berries (ask your florist to order them or purchase a simulated version)*
- *rose hips (wear gloves and watch for thorns!)*
- *pepperberries*
- *2 grapevine wreath frames of different sizes (we used a 6-inch frame and a 12-inch frame)*
- *a spool of florist's wire*
- *wire cutters*
- *ribbon for a bow*

Start with the larger grapevine form. Prepare tallow-berry clusters by separating them carefully into small bunches of three to four sprigs each. Fasten wire onto the wreath. Lay a bunch of berries on the wreath form, and attach with a loose loop of wire wound around. Repeat with another bunch of berries placed directly below, going around and around the form. Completely cover the front and sides of the form with berry bunches. When finished, secure the wire in back with a hidden knot. Repeat with the smaller wreath. Set inside the larger wreath, secure with wire, and add a bow. Attach a small wire hook to the back of the larger form for hanging your finished masterpiece.

(206)

★ crafts

131

Trim the tree with **handcrafted** treasures.

207. Make ribbon ornaments inspired by old-fashioned ribbon candy. For each ornament you will need:

- *2 glass beads*
- *lightweight fishing line*
- *a sewing needle*
- *½ yard of 2-inch-wide wire-edged ribbon*

To make the ornaments: String fishing line through a bead, then around and through again, forming a loop. Leave about 12 inches of line on the other side and cut. String the line through a needle and put aside. Fold one raw edge of ribbon under, then continue folding 2-inch sections accordion style to create 5 to 6 loops. Fold the last raw edge under. Run the needle with line through the center of the ribbon, then through the second bead and form a loop around it. (Loops allow tension to be created, so ribbons can open up a bit wider.) Tie a piece of fishing line to one bead on the ornament and tie to tree, then tie a smaller piece of ribbon around fishing line to cover it.

208. For a more delicate version of the paper chain, make a ribbon chain. Choose narrow ribbons in an assortment of colors, cut into 4-inch pieces, then glue the ends in a circle, one after the other, to the desired length.

209. Embellish a starfish with buttons.

crafts

★

133

(211)

210. Victorian calling cards give a tree the romantic look of a bygone era. Make color photocopies of antique cards, or purchase reproductaions, and glue the copies to a sturdy paper background. String them with satin cords and decorate with pearl and crystal beads.

211. Craft a rustic star ornament. With a craft knife, cut a star from found birch bark (never strip it from trees). Glue found twigs painted gold to the bark, wind 20-gauge gold wire around one point, and twist it until it's secured to the branch.

(210)

212. Use your collection of fabric scraps to craft rag ball ornaments. You will need:

- *Styrofoam balls (all one size or in a variety of sizes)*
- *pins*
- *fabric strips of any kind*
- *felt shapes (cut them yourself or purchase them at a fabric shop)*
- *ribbon or trim for hanging them on the tree*

To make: Stick a pin through a strip of fabric at a starting point on a Styrofoam ball. Continue wrapping the ball with the fabric strips, using pins to hold them in place, until the ball is completely covered. You can adhere the fabric randomly or arrange it in a more orderly design. To embellish the balls with felt shapes, string a pin with a bead, then push the pin through the felt into the ball. Attach a loop of ribbon or trim to the top of the ball with a pin.

Colorful papers, **rainbow ribbons**, and **whimsical** touches turn presents into **presentations**.

213. Give new purpose to buttons by using them as embellishments on your holiday packages. Here, a wired spray of buttons decorates citrus-inspired ribbons and wrapping paper.

214. Think outside the box and run ribbons lengthwise across gifts, instead of the classic crisscross.

215

MINERAL
SPECIMENS

215. Make a personal statement and add distinctive flair when wrapping holiday gifts. Finish packaging them with bakery string, twine, or decorative ribbon such as textured grosgrain, silky satin, crisp taffeta, or luminous sheer (available at fabric, craft, or hardware stores). Cut wide ribbons with pinking shears to create a decorative edge.

216. The perfect marriage of present and presentation can yield a small work of art, suitable for display around the holidays or at any time of year. These diminutive ornaments of blue, green, and gold, packaged in a vintage glass-top box that was once used to hold mineral specimens is a perfect example.

217. Give vintage wallpaper new life as wrapping paper. Stiffer than traditional wrapping paper, wallpaper requires extra manipulation to achieve crisp corners. Old paper can also be brittle, so have extra adhesive tape on hand to reinforce small tears. Vintage wallpaper rolls frequently turn up at flea markets, on eBay, and in antiques shops.

218. Use brown paper and red string, tied in a variety of ways, and an exquisite ornament to create a memorable presentation.

219. Plain paper goods become novel name tags with the help of a hole puncher. The brown-and-white coasters shown here are a case in point. Other ideas include bookplates, place cards, vintage postcards, and the self-adhesive labels used for jelly jars.

220. Newspaper, especially foreign language papers, make wonderful gift wrapping. Gussy them up with colorful trimmings.

221. For a bit of Old World charm, wrap presents in sheet music or photo-copied pages from vintage books. Used-book stores often carry inexpensive music and volumes that are damaged but retain usable individual sheets. Choosing favorite composers or authors will personalize the gifts.

222. For an easy gift tag, use an indelible metallic-ink marker to inscribe the recipient's name directly onto a fabric ribbon.

223. When packing presents to mail or to carry, bows can get crushed. Instead of using a bow, affix a beautiful card to the wrapping paper.

224. A handmade box is as much a present as what's inside. To craft these gift boxes you'll need:

- *fabric or wallpaper to photocopy*
- *a glue stick, cardboard*
- *card stock*
- *a ruler and pencil*
- *a small round object to trace*
- *scissors*
- *scallop-edged scissors (optional)*

To make: Photocopy a piece of fabric or wallpaper onto card stock. Measure and cut lengthwise the desired height of the box's body, then glue the ends together to form a round body. Trace a round object slightly larger than the opening of the body to make the top and bottom, and cut each piece with scallop-edged scissors. Cut cardboard into 4 strips, each about 2 inches long by $\frac{1}{2}$ inch wide and fold in half. Glue the strips to the inside bottom of the box and against the sides to adhere the bottom to the sides. Cut a small hole in the top of the box, form a piece of ribbon into a loop, and knot under the box top for a handle. Fill with light-weight treats.

225. It's the finishing touches that add elegance to your gifts. Several hues of blue in different textures; handmade paper fastened with crystal pushpins, an airy organza bow embellished with crystal teardrop ornaments, and crystal beaded garlanding entwined around the ribbon, add a touch of holiday romance to a present.

226. To prevent ribbons from fraying, cut the edges with pinking shears, or make a tiny knot at each end of the ribbon so it can only fray a little.

227. Embellish your gifts with a seashell instead of a traditional bow.

228. In addition to hand-tied ribbons, experiment with fresh flowers or greenery, costume jewelry, flea-market ornaments, and big, glittery cardboard monograms.

229. Make a felt gift bag. Cut two rectangles of felt (use two different colors); stitch the rectangles together on three sides, leaving one side open. Tuck a present into the bag and tie it shut with ribbon. Or make a pouch by cutting one rectangle about five inches longer than the other rectangle to create a flap that can be folded over. Scallop the edge of the top flap and secure with a button or ribbon. Decorate with felt cutouts.

230. Personalize gift tags with rubber stamps, holiday stickers, and other items available in stationery and craft stores. Secure each to a box using a length of vintage ribbon, bakery string, or jewel-toned embroidery thread.

Deck the halls with **handmade** holiday decorations.

(232)

231. Use your fabric scraps to create one-of-a-kind stockings.

(231)

232. Use newspaper to turn a glass vessel into an artistic decoration. Measure the height or width of the glass and cut strips of newspaper to fit. Brush water-based glue onto the glass, and affix strips, adding pictures, bold letters, or heartfelt words. Brush on another thin layer of glue to seal.

(233)

235. Whimsical flatware holders can be made for each place setting. Cut out two white stocking shapes and sew them together with ecru embroidery thread and glue a strip of ecru felt across the top.

233. Create a scalloped trim for your holiday mantel display. The scalloped edging was created by cutting felt 3-inches wide with scalloped pinking shears. Attach silver dragées (the kind used to decorate cookies) to the scalloped edge with a hot glue gun, and secure the felt to the mantel with double-faced tape.

234. Christmas pins are wearable art, but they also make festive decorative accents. They can adorn pillows, curtains, and ribbons. They can also be displayed on small feather trees as ornaments or used to embellish wrapped gifts. Here, a selection of Swarovski Christmas-tree pins sits prettily on a red velvet ribbon bulletin board frame to dress up a display of vintage cards.

(234)

(235)

(236)

236. With a little bit of glue and a lot of imagination, white baby socks can be transformed into tiny snowmen by stuffing them and tying them with ribbon. This is an ideal holiday project for children.

237. Place cards can be crafted from last year's greeting cards. Using a dove-shaped cookie cutter, trace a silhouette onto the printed side of the card. On the opposite side, stamp or handwrite the name of your guest. Display in a pinecone.

(237)

Merry Christmas Jonathon

★ crafts

151

238. Let it snow! Assure yourself a flurry of snowflakes by getting a little crafty with tissue paper and scissors. No time to snip? Ask an artistic friend to help, or use store-bought paper snowflakes. To display them in the window, spritz the panes (inside the house) with water using a plant mister or a recycled spray bottle filled with plain water. Place the cutouts on the misted window and voilà! The faux flakes will stay in place, looking festive for weeks inside and out.

239. Bring a sense of the past to your home by handcrafting folk-art decorations. To make these votives, tape a small paper tree to the glass, spray the entire glass with glue, and roll it in artificial snow or glitter so that it looks frosted. When the paper is removed, the tree will be transparent, allowing a colored candle within to glimmer through. After the holidays, the Christmas motif can be washed off with hot, soapy water.

240. Create a pinecone tree on a cone-shaped foam base. Anchor the base in a container, then wire the cones onto 2-inch wooden floral picks. Insert picks downward into the foam, starting at the bottom with the largest cones and working to the top with the smaller ones. Conceal the foam by tucking sheet moss among the pinecones.

241. Transform your old cashmere sweaters into the prettiest stockings ever.

crafts

242. Use leftover scraps of felt to make a garland. Here, a garland made of rough-cut squares of white and off-white felt interspersed with small bells is strung along a mantel beside ornaments and a trio of neutral-toned Christmas stockings.

243. Make your own tiered stand for sweets. With glass glue, adhere the base of a candlestick to the bottom of a luncheon plate. Turn a second candlestick upside down and glue it to the bottom of a saucer. Place a book on top of the saucer and let set for about 20 minutes, then pile on the goodies.

244. Make a fanciful conical rib-bon-wrapped "tree". You'll need:

- *Styrofoam cones (in assorted sizes up to 24 inches)*
- *Ribbons in assorted widths*
- *Braid and trim*
- *Straight pins with decorative heads, especially 2-inch corsage pins*
- *Beads and other faux jewels*

With a straight pin, secure one end of a 2-inch wide and 1½-yard long ribbon to the top of a cone. Overlapping the edges, wrap the ribbon diagonally, fastening with pins every four inches. Secure the end with a pin under the base. Skewer beads with corsage pins to create festive patterns (like these snowflakes) or decorate randomly. For the best results, insert pins into the cone at a slightly downward angle. (Tip: A decorative hatpin makes a stellar topper.) Add braid, pearls, beads, baubles, and other sparkling embellishments as lavishly as desired. For a finished look—and a touch of chic!—decorate the top, and pin a border of fringe, braid, or trim along the base. Stand the tree on its base, or place it on a pedestal for extra height.

(244)

(245)

247. To make simple Christmas "crackers," gather cardboard paper rolls, fill with trinkets, wrap in newsprint, and tie the ends with ribbon. They may not pop when opened, but they will spill with goodies. When accented with a monogrammed tag, these become both place cards and party favors.

(247)

245. Fashion napkin rings using buttons, beads, and ruby jewelry.

246. Create a dazzling centerpiece by adding colorful beads to a plain pillar candle, then surround it with glittered ornaments affixed with glue to a carboard wreath form.

(246)

251. Embellish plain pillar candles. Using a hot glue gun or tiny pushpins, decorate with berries, holly leaves, glitter, confetti, cinnamon sticks, or pine needles.

248. Give the gift of scent. Make a paper cone from construction paper; secure it with tape or glue. Decorate the cone with stickers or rubber stamps. Cut a piece of tulle to fit inside, and fill with lavender. Punch two holes at the top to string a ribbon through them for hanging.

249. Make a star garland. Using one star as a template, cut out as many as desired. Punch a small hole in the center of each star and string with thin twine. Drape around a tree, across a window, or along a banister.

250. Search out vintage postcards at flea markets, secure them to twine with clips and string them across a mirror.

253. Craft a ribbon-trimmed cake stand for a holiday gathering. Measure and cut enough heavyweight cream-colored paper to cover one side a 5-inch Styrofoam disk. Secure the paper with straight pins. Trace a 10-inch foil-covered cake base top onto the paper, cut out, and glue to the foil top. With a hot glue gun, secure the Styrofoam disk to the center of the cake top on the underside. Measure and cut a piece (or two) of paper to fit around the rim of the cake top. Trim the bottom edge of the paper using decorative-edged scissors. Attach the paper to the rim of the cake top with pins. Then measure, cut, and glue 2-inch wide striped ribbon to the top portion of the paper-covered rim and to the bottom of the disk. For a larger cake stand, use a 12-inch foil-covered cake base top and $\frac{1}{2}$-inch ribbon.

254. Fashion stockings using vintage tablecloths printed with holiday motifs. Here, the initials are cut from vintage handkerchiefs. (The middle stocking was made of felt.)

252. Embellish the shelves in an armoire or closet. Measure the shelves and mark the length on a $3\frac{1}{2}$-inch wide to $4\frac{1}{2}$-inch wide piece of heavyweight cream-colored paper. Turn a dessert plate or saucer upside down onto the edge of the paper and trace it halfway around to form a semicircle. With a ruler, draw a triangle next to the circle. Alternate the semicircle and triangles along the length of the paper leaving a $\frac{1}{2}$-inch wide margin at the top so the two shapes connect. Cut out patterns then attach to shelf edges with double-sided tape.

256. Use paper place mats or construction paper cut with a scalloped border to make a menu holder that hangs on the back of a chair. Using a glue stick, affix the front of a large holiday card to the sides and bottom of the card to form a pocket to hold a menu for the holiday meal. You can use the smooth back of a lovely card front for the menu, too. Hang the menu holder from the back of a chair with colorful ribbon, threaded through two punched holes.

255. Craft paper birdhouses from recycled milk cartons and greeting cards. In this case, reproduction Victorian greeting cards are illustrated with wintry scenes.

To make: Open both ends of a pint-size milk carton top. Wrap a blank sheet of paper around carton and secure with tape. Make folds in the paper where the carton is scored. Use this as a template for cutting silk paper. Cut the silk paper and fold where scored on the carton. Glue into place with a gluestick. Tape two postcards together, scallop the edges, and fold in half. Pinch the top of the milk carton together; place taped postcards over the top to form a roof. Punch a hole through the postcards and carton, thread a length of ribbon through, and tie closed.

257. Steal a smooch under a charming kissing ball. Composed of Lady apples and fresh cranberries mounted on a sphere of Styrofoam and dusted with sparkling sugar, this easy-to-make arrangement will delight for weeks.

You'll need:
- *Letter opener*
- *24 inches of ribbon*
- *8-inch or 10-inch Styrofoam ball*
- *Floral picks (with wire removed) and toothpicks*
- *Approximately 40 Lady apples and 60 fresh cranberries*
- *Pastry brush*
- *2 egg whites, lightly beaten*
- *1 cup sugar*
- *Baking rack*

To make: Using a letter opener, feed the ribbon through the center of a Styrofoam ball. Tie the ribbon into a bow at one end and leave it slack at the other. Secure the ribbon by inserting a floral pick at the knot. Push the blunt end of a floral pick a quarter of the way into the bottom of a Lady apple, then push the pointed end all the way into the Styrofoam ball. Cover the entire ball with apples, then spear cranberries onto toothpicks and fill in the spaces. Use a pastry brush to paint the apples and cranberries with egg whites. Place on a baking rack for about 15 minutes, or until the egg white is nearly dry but still tacky. Sprinkle sugar over entire surface of the ball, then place on a rack until dry. Shake off the excess sugar, hang the ball over a doorway, and enjoy!

258. Make a wreath using holiday cards. Simply use a hot glue gun to attach cards to a wreath form and hang with a festive bow.

259. Give the gift of food to your feathered friends outdoors by providing them with home-made peanut rings. To make, thread unshelled peanuts at their narrowest point onto lengths of thin galvanized wire (for a large ring, you'll need about 15 inches of wire). Bend the wire to form a good-size circle, then twist the ends together tightly to secure them. Hang the ring with house-hold twine.

(258)

(259)

260. Make a Christmas tree for the birds. This can be as simple as propping a handful of wintry branches in an old watering can and decorating them with peeled apples. Other edible decorations might include pinecones rolled in peanut butter and birdseed.

four

Baking

The holidays are a baker's dream come true. Baking is a cherished holiday tradition, and come December, visions of fanciful cookies and luscious cakes become a reality. From beautifully iced sugar cookies to elaborately decorated gingerbread men, decorating dozens upon dozens of cookies is as much a part of the holidays as brightly wrapped presents and twinkling lights. It simply wouldn't be Christmas without cookies, as they're often the high point at holiday gatherings and make tempting presents for favorite teachers and neighbors alike. Make a gift of cookies even more memorable by packing them in distinctive containers. Arrange them in a vintage lunchbox, tuck them into a colorfully decorated cigar box, or stack them in a simple tin canister festively tied with ribbon. Elegantly wrapped, cookies also make sweet party favors, allowing guests to enjoy the occasion long after it's over. Cakes also make the holidays special. They are often the star of the holiday buffet table, whether a scrumptiously rich chocolate cake or a fluffy white coconut confection. On the following pages you'll find an enticing selection of the season's best-loved cakes and cookies. Enjoy their tempting aroma and buttery flavor, but be sure to leave some for Santa on Christmas Eve. After all, cookies are what sweet memories are all about.

Nestle homemade treats in pretty packaging.

263. Make your baked gift extra-special by including a handmade or computer-designed recipe card.

264. As an alternative to traditional paper cards, present friends and loved ones with edible Christmas "card" trees decorated with royal icing. Package them in clear cellophane envelopes fastened with festive ribbons.

261. Homemade treats are even more special when they arrive in a distinctive container. This 1950s school lunch box, with latching lid and its original handle, is a collector's dream.

262. Create a personalized gift bag. Stack cutout cookies in a baking cup encircled with a matching ribbon. Place the filled cup into a "cello" bag and, using pinking shears, make a zigzag cut across the top of the bag. String a copy of the recipe and a glittery initial of the recipient on a ribbon and secure bag with a bow.

265. Before placing edibles in any vintage container, be sure it's thoroughly clean and dry. To clean and disinfect tin cans, add a few drops of bleach to hot, soapy water, then wash, rinse thoroughly, and dry well. Seal wood, cardboard, or papier-mâché boxes with water-based polyurethane.

266. Think beyond conventional baskets—almost any unusual container can enhance a gift of cookies, cakes, or holiday sweets. Vintage cigar boxes (1900–1950) are sought after by collectors for their colorful lithographed labels and unusual graphics.

267. Revive antique chocolate and candy tins (these are from the 1940s and '50s) for holiday treats now, and for holding jewelry, trinkets, or buttons later. To freshen the interiors, paint them with chrome-colored spray paint. When thoroughly dry, line the tins with napkins, tissue paper, fabric, or doilies.

268. Even the most unassuming container, such as a humble tin can, can have unexpected charm when sashed with a red raffia tie and bejeweled with a 1920s tree ornament of mercury glass. The cookies are nestled in crimped parchment paper.

269. When it comes to gift containers for homemade treats, almost anything works. Here a Victorian silverplate tobacco caddy holds pecan cookies wrapped in "gingham" tissue.

270. Use a vintage lunchbox tied with a pretty bow and greenery to "wrap" a gift of cookies.

271. Nestle a gift of homemade cookies and cookie cutters in a tea towel inside a pretty green-and-white picnic-plaid tin.

272. To keep baked goods fresh when shipping, wrap in foil or plastic wrap; be sure to label before packing. Cookies or bars should be individually wrapped or packed in layers with waxed paper or tissue in between.

baking

★

'Tis the season for **baking holiday** cookies.

273. Chocolate Snowflakes

Snowflake-shaped cookie cutters give these cookies their authentic look.

Makes about 6 dozen cookies

4½ cups all-purpose flour

⅔ cup Dutch-processed unsweetened cocoa

1½ teaspoons ground cinnamon

½ teaspoon salt

2 cups unsalted butter (4 sticks), softened

1¼ cups sugar

2 large eggs

2 large egg yolks

2 teaspoons vanilla extract

6 ounces white chocolate, melted

2 teaspoons vegetable shortening, melted

1. Make the dough: Sift the flour, cocoa, cinnamon, and salt together into a medium bowl. Set aside. Beat the butter in a large bowl using a mixer set on medium speed until creamy. Gradually add the sugar and continue to beat until incorporated. Add the eggs, yolks, and vanilla and beat thoroughly.

Pictured, clockwise from top right: Coffee-Cream Sandwiches (page 201), Pistachio-Cranberry Stacks (page 195), Spritz (page 194), Holiday Blondies (page 196), Double-Chocolate Snowquakes (page 199), Caramel Thumbprints (page 190), Mini Thumbprints with Currant Jam (page 191), and Chocolate Snowflakes (this page).

Reduce the mixer speed to medium-low and add the flour mixture and beat until a soft dough forms. Divide the dough in half. Shape each piece into a 6- by 4-inch rectangle, wrap each in plastic wrap, and refrigerate for 4 to 24 hours.

2. Cut out the cookies: Preheat the oven to 350°F. Line 2 baking sheets with parchment paper. On a lightly floured surface, roll the dough out to ⅛-inch thickness. With a snowflake-shaped cookie cutter, cut out cookies and place, 2 inches apart, on the prepared baking sheets. Chill for 10 to 15 minutes. Gather up the dough scraps, form into a disk, and rechill. Repeat to make more cookies.

3. Bake the cookies: Bake the cookies, rotating the baking sheets halfway through the baking until firm to the touch—about 12 minutes. Transfer the cookies to wire racks to cool completely. Store the undecorated cookies in an airtight container for up to 1 week.

4. Decorate the cookies: Mix the white chocolate and vegetable shortening together. Transfer the mixture to a pastry bag fitted with a small plain tip and pipe designs onto the cookies. Allow the chocolate to set—about 15 minutes. The decorated cookies will keep, layered between waxed paper, in an airtight container for up to 3 days.

274. Checkerboard Cookies

Checkerboard cookies look difficult to make but they really aren't. It is simply a matter of slicing and stacking the layers of chocolate and vanilla dough. Once you try making them, you are sure to get hooked!

Makes 6 dozen cookies

5 cups all-purpose flour, sifted

1/4 teaspoon salt

2 cups unsalted butter (4 sticks), softened

1 cup sugar

2 large eggs

2 teaspoons vanilla extract

3 tablespoons Dutch-processed unsweetened cocoa

1 large egg white

1. Make the dough: Combine the flour and salt in a medium bowl. Set aside. Beat the butter in a large bowl using a mixer set on medium-high speed until light and creamy. Gradually add the sugar and continue to beat until light and fluffy. Add the eggs one at a time, beating well after each addition. Add the vanilla. Reduce the mixer speed to low and beat in the flour mixture until a dough forms. Remove half the dough and set aside. Mix the cocoa into the remaining dough until fully incorporated. Pat the vanilla and the chocolate dough into 11- by 9-inch rectangles. Wrap each in plastic wrap and chill until firm.

2. Make the checkerboards: Brush the vanilla dough with egg white and place the chocolate dough on top. Press gently and cut in half lengthwise. Brush one half with egg white and stack the remaining half on top, making certain the vanilla and chocolate doughs alternate. Cut the resulting stack in half lengthwise and set one stack aside. Slice one stack into thirds lengthwise and flip the middle stack over; lightly brush the sides with egg white and gently press together to form a checkerboard-patterned log. Wrap in plastic wrap and chill until firm. Repeat with the remaining stack.

3. Bake the cookies: Preheat the oven to 350° F. Line 2 baking sheets with parchment paper. Slice 1 checkerboard log crosswise into 1/4-inch-thick cookies. Place 1 inch apart on the prepared baking sheets and bake, rotating the sheets halfway through, until firm—12 to 15 minutes. Transfer the cookies to wire racks to cool completely. Store in an airtight container for up to 1 week.

275. Bake only if you have the time and truly enjoy it. Otherwise, buy sugar cookies at the bakery and dress them up with icing, embellish gingerbread men with frosting "rickrack", and decorate with pieces of taffeta ribbon to make them even more appealing.

276. Pecan Butter Cookies

To make these cookies (seen here on the left) even more delectable, dip one corner into melted dark chocolate to dress them up.

Makes 5 dozen cookies

4 cups all-purpose flour, sifted

1 teaspoon salt

2 cups unsalted butter (4 sticks), softened

1 cup firmly packed light brown sugar

1½ teaspoons vanilla extract

2 cups pecans, toasted and chopped

4 ounces bittersweet chocolate, chopped

2 tablespoons unsalted butter, cut into small pieces

TIP: After toasting the nuts, let them **cool completely** before chopping or processing.

1. Make the dough: Combine the flour and salt in a small bowl. Set aside. Beat the 2 cups butter and brown sugar in a large bowl using an electric mixer set on medium speed until light and fluffy—about 2 minutes. Add the vanilla. Reduce the mixer speed to low and beat in the flour mixture. Stir in the nuts. Divide the dough into 4 equal pieces, wrap in plastic wrap, and chill for 1 hour. Shape the dough into 4 logs and chill until cold—at least 2 hours. The dough can be frozen at this point for up to 2 months.

2. Bake the cookies: Preheat the oven to 350°F. Line 2 baking sheets with parchment paper. Slice the logs on an angle into ¼-inch-thick rounds and place, about 1 inch apart, on the prepared baking sheets. Bake until golden brown—about 15 minutes. Transfer the cookies to wire racks to cool.

3. Dip the cookies: Set a wire rack over a sheet of waxed paper. Set aside. Fill a saucepan with 1 inch of water and bring to a boil. Reduce the heat to medium-low. Combine the chocolate and pieces of butter in a metal bowl and set over the boiling water. Cook, stirring occasionally until melted and well blended. Remove the bowl from the heat. Dip one edge of the cookies, one at a time, into the melted chocolate and shake off the excess. Place on wire racks until set—about 30 minutes.

277. Spitzbuebe

These cookies require a little extra work but are so elegant that they're worth it. The star cut-out in the center of the top layer shows off the layer of jam inside.

Makes 4 dozen cookies

2 cups unsalted butter (4 sticks), softened

4 cups plus 2 tablespoons confectioners' sugar

4 large egg yolks

4 2/3 cups all-purpose flour

1 cup seedless jam, warmed until syrupy

1. Make the dough: Beat the butter in a large bowl using an electric mixer set on medium speed until creamy. Gradually add 4 cups confectioners' sugar and continue to beat until light and fluffy—5 to 8 minutes. Beat in the yolks, one at a time, then stir in the flour. Shape the dough into four ½-inch-thick squares and wrap each in plastic wrap. Chill for at least 45 minutes.

2. Bake the cookies: Preheat the oven to 350°F. Line 2 baking sheets with parchment paper. Set aside. Roll the dough out on a lightly floured surface to ¼-inch thickness. With a 2-inch round cookie cutter, cut out rounds, then use a star cutter to punch out the centers on half the rounds. Place the rounds, 1 inch apart, on prepared baking sheets. Reduce the oven temperature to 325°F and bake until golden—about 15 minutes. Repeat with remaining dough and dough scraps. Transfer the cookies to wire racks to cool completely. Spoon ¼ teaspoon jam on the solid cookies. Dust the cut-out cookies with the remaining confectioners' sugar. Place the cut-out cookies on top of the jam-topped cookies. Store, layered between sheets of wax paper, in an airtight container for up to 1 week.

TIP: Substitute ready-made refrigerated cookie dough and skip step 1.

278. Lemon Meringue Cookies

For formal parties, use an antique compote or crystal punch bowl to display your most special sweets to spectacular effect. Our meringue cookies, tinted with edible sparkling dust, emulate the shape and glow of vintage ornaments.

Makes about 3 dozen cookies

6 large egg whites, at room temperature

2 teaspoons fresh lemon juice

$\frac{1}{8}$ teaspoon salt

1 teaspoon lemon extract

1 teaspoon vanilla extract

1$\frac{1}{4}$ cups sugar

1. Make the meringues: Preheat the oven to 200°F. Line 2 baking sheets with parchment paper. Combine the egg whites, lemon juice, and salt in a large bowl and beat using a mixer set on low speed until foamy. Add the extracts, increase the mixer speed to medium, and add the sugar in a slow, continuous stream. Increase speed to medium-high and continue to beat until stiff peaks form.

2. Bake the cookies: Transfer the meringue to a large pastry bag fitted with a large star tip. Pipe 3-inch "S" shapes on the prepared baking sheets. Bake, without opening the oven, for 1 hour. Reduce the temperature to 175°F and continue to bake for 2 more hours or until cookies are completely dry. Transfer the cookies, on the parchment paper, to wire racks to cool completely. Store in an airtight container for up to 1 week.

279. Simple Sugar Cookies

It wouldn't be Christmas without this traditional favorite, cut as stars, candy canes, ornaments, and Christmas trees and decorated as simply or as elaborately as you like. (See photo on page 182.)

(See photo on page 182.)

Makes about 4 dozen cookies

5 cups all-purpose flour

³/₄ teaspoon ground nutmeg

¹/₂ teaspoon salt

2 cups unsalted butter (4 sticks), room temperature

1¹/₄ cups granulated sugar

2 large eggs

2 large egg yolks

2 teaspoons vanilla extract

1 large egg white, lightly beaten

Colored sugars for sprinkling

1. Make the dough: Combine the flour, nutmeg, and salt in a medium bowl. Set aside. Beat the butter in a large bowl using a mixer set on medium speed, until creamy and fluffy. Gradually add the granulated sugar and beat until light and fluffy. Add the eggs, egg yolks, and vanilla and beat thoroughly. Reduce the mixer speed to medium low, add the flour mixture, and beat until a dough forms. Divide the dough in half, shape each piece into a 6- by 4-inch rectangle, and wrap in plastic wrap. Chill for 4 to 24 hours.

2. Bake the cookies: Preheat the oven to 350°F. Line 2 baking sheets with parchment paper. On a lightly floured surface, roll out the dough to ¹/₈-inch thickness. Cut out shapes of your choice with cookie cutters and place 2 inches apart, on the prepared baking sheets. Lightly brush the cookies with the egg white, sprinkle with colored sugar, and shake off any excess. Bake, rotating the baking sheets halfway through, until the cookies are golden brown—about 15 minutes. Transfer the cookies to wire racks to cool completely. Gather up the dough scraps, form into a disk, and rechill. Repeat to make more cookies. Store in an airtight container for up to 1 week.

280. Chocolate-Mint Sandwich Cookies

These sublime cookies have a delectable chocolate-mint filling, making them seem extra-special and just perfect for the holidays.

Makes 3 dozen cookies

1 cup all-purpose flour

1 tablespoon unsweetened cocoa

$\frac{1}{2}$ cup cold unsalted butter (1 stick), cut into 8 pieces

$\frac{1}{2}$ cup heavy cream

$1\frac{1}{2}$ cups plus 2 tablespoons confectioners' sugar

6 tablespoons unsalted butter, softened

1 teaspoon vanilla extract

16 thin chocolate mints, finely chopped ($\frac{1}{2}$ cup)

1. Make the dough: Combine the flour, cocoa, and butter in the bowl of a food processor fitted with the metal blade and pulse until the mixture resembles coarse meal. With the processor running, gradually add $\frac{1}{4}$ cup heavy cream and process until a dough forms. Shape the dough into a disk. Wrap in plastic wrap and chill for 1 hour.

2. Bake the cookies: Preheat oven to 375°F. Line a baking sheet with parchment paper. Set aside. Lightly dust a work surface with the 2 tablespoons confectioners' sugar and roll the dough to $\frac{1}{8}$-inch thickness. Using a $1\frac{1}{4}$-inch round cookie cutter, cut out the cookies and place 1 inch apart on the prepared baking sheet. Use a fork to prick 3 rows of holes into each cookie. Bake until firm to the touch—8 to 10 minutes. Cool on the baking sheet or a wire rack for 5 minutes. Transfer the cookies to a wire rack to cool completely.

3. Assemble the cookies: Beat the softened butter and $1\frac{1}{2}$ cups confectioners' sugar in a small bowl using a mixer set on medium speed. Add the remaining cream and the vanilla and beat until smooth. Stir in the chocolate mints. Spread 2 teaspoons filling on the bottoms of half the cookies and cover with the tops of the cookies. Store in an airtight container for up to 3 days.

Pictured on the left, Chocolate-Mint Sandwich Cookies; on the right, Simple Sugar Cookies (page 181).

281. Candy Cane Cookies

Use a double batch of our Simple Sugar Cookies recipe on page 181. Roll the dough out to ¼-inch thickness and bake the cookies for 18 to 20 minutes to make these dramatic cookie ornaments.

Makes about 32 cookies

4–5 cups confectioners' sugar

¼ cup meringue powder

4–6 tablespoons water

32 large candy cane cookies

1. Make the icing: Beat 4 cups confectioners' sugar, the meringue powder, and 4 tablespoons water in a large bowl using a mixer set on low speed until smooth. Increase the speed to medium-high and continue to beat until the icing thickens and holds its shape for about 10 seconds when the beaters are lifted. If necessary, add more confectioners' sugar to stiffen or water to loosen the icing to achieve the desired consistency. Transfer about one-third of the icing to a medium bowl and color with red food coloring. Cover both the white and the red icing with plastic wrap until ready to use.

2. Decorate the cookies: Place a wire rack over sheets of waxed paper and place cookies, about 1½ inches apart, on the rack. Use a ½-inch paintbrush to thickly coat the top and sides of each cookie with white icing. Clean away any hanging icing drips and transfer to clean sheets of waxed paper to dry—about 12 hours. Fill a pastry bag fitted with a small round tip (#2 or 3) with red icing. Beginning at the top of each cookie, pipe lines to simulate a candy cane pattern. Fill in the wider spaced lines with the red icing. Allow to dry thoroughly—about 24 hours.

282. Gingerbread Boys

Baking gingerbread cakes and cookies dates back to eleventh-century Europe. Of all the countries, however, Germany has the grandest tradition of baking shaped gingerbread cookies.

Makes about 30 cookies

3 cups all-purpose flour

1 tablespoon ground ginger

2 teaspoons ground cinnamon

1½ teaspoons baking powder

¾ teaspoon baking soda

¼ teaspoon ground nutmeg

¼ teaspoon salt

6 tablespoons butter (¾ stick), softened

¼ cup firmly packed dark brown sugar

1 large egg

¼ cup dark molasses

2 teaspoons vanilla extract

Ready-to-use white icing (optional)

Silver dragées (optional)

1. Make the dough: Combine flour, ginger, cinnamon, baking powder, baking soda, nutmeg, and salt in a medium bowl. Set aside.

2. Beat the butter and brown sugar in a large bowl using an electric mixer, set on medium speed, until light and fluffy. Beat in the egg, molasses, and vanilla. Reduce the mixer speed to low, gradually add the flour mixture and beat until a stiff dough forms. Divide the dough in half and shape each piece into a ball. Wrap each ball in plastic wrap and let stand at room temperature for 1 hour.

3. Bake the cookies: Preheat the oven to 350°F. Lightly grease 2 baking sheets. Line the baking sheets with waxed paper and lightly flour. Roll out 1 ball of dough out between pieces of waxed paper to ¼-inch thickness. Remove the top piece of waxed paper. Using a 3½-inch gingerbread boy cookie cutter, cut out as many cookies as possible, leaving a ¾-inch space between each cookie. Remove all the scraps and press together. Invert the waxed paper with the gingerbread boys onto a prepared baking sheet and peel off the waxed paper. Bake the cookies until the edges are slightly darkened—7 to 10 minutes. Let cool on the baking sheets on wire racks for 5 minutes. Transfer the cookies to wire racks to cool completely. Roll out, cut, and bake the remaining ball of dough and dough scraps to make more cookies. Use the white icing and silver dragées to decorate cookies as desired. Store in an airtight container for up to 1 week.

283. Christmas Shortbread

Buttery, crumbly shortbread is always a welcome treat. To bake up perfect shortbread, don't over-beat the butter and sugars and mix in the flour just until blended.

Makes 16 pieces

¾ cup unsalted butter (1½ sticks), softened

⅓ cup confectioners' sugar

2 tablespoons granulated sugar

¼ teaspoon salt

1½ cups all-purpose flour

1. Make the dough: Preheat the oven to 350°F. Beat the butter, both sugars, and salt in a medium bowl with an electric mixer on medium speed, until well blended. Sift the flour into the bowl with the butter mixture. Reduce the mixer speed to low and beat just until a stiff dough forms.

2. Using your fingertips, firmly press the dough onto the bottom of an ungreased 9-inch cake pan, forming a compact, even layer. Using the tip of a knife, score the dough into 16 triangles, being careful not to cut all the way through. Using the tines of a fork, pierce the dough all over in a decorative pattern.

3. Bake the shortbread: Bake until the shortbread is lightly browned—35 to 40 minutes. Remove from the oven and immediately cut into wedges along the scored lines. Place the pan on a wire rack to cool completely. Store the shortbread in an airtight container for up to 1 week.

284. Coconut Cookie Favors

Send guests home with delectables set in silver paper cups, individually wrapped in cellophane, and tied up with satin ribbons.

Makes 2 dozen cookies

2 cups sweetened flaked coconut

¼ cup sugar

1½ tablespoons all-purpose flour

4 tablespoons butter (½ stick), melted

2 large egg yolks

1 large egg

Preheat the oven to 350° F. Line a baking sheet with parchment paper. Set aside. Toss the coconut, sugar, flour, butter, egg yolks, and egg together in a large bowl. Mix well. With wet hands, form the mixture into walnut-size balls, and place on the prepared baking sheet. Bake until lightly golden—about 12 to 15 minutes. Transfer the cookies to wire racks to cool completely.

285. Red-and-White Mcringues

An easy-to-prepare meringue makes light and delicious cookies, especially perfect after a day of holiday indulgences.

Makes about 50 meringues

6 large egg whites, at room temperature

2 teaspoons fresh lemon juice

1/8 teaspoon salt

1/2 teaspoon peppermint extract

1/2 teaspoon vanilla extract

1 1/4 cups sugar

Red food coloring

1. Make the meringue: Preheat the oven to 200° F. Line 2 baking sheets with parchment paper. Set aside. Combine the egg whites, lemon juice, and salt in a large bowl, and beat using a mixer set on low until foamy. Beat in the peppermint and vanilla extracts; beat until combined. Add sugar in a slow stream. Increase the mixer speed to medium-high. Continue to beat until stiff, glossy peaks form. Do not overbeat. Transfer half the meringue to a large bowl. Set aside. Reduce the mixer speed to low. Beat in enough red food coloring to the remaining meringue to get the desired color. Do not overbeat.

2. Bake the meringues: Put a large pastry bag fitted with a 1/2-inch plain tip in a large glass and fold the top of the piping bag over the rim of the glass. Using two large spoons, simultaneously drop dollops of the white meringue and red meringue into the piping bag, side by side. Continue adding the two meringues until they reach three-fourths of the way up the glass. Remove the pastry bag from the glass, fold the sides of the bag up, and twist to seal. Pipe 1 1/2-inch mounds onto the prepared baking sheets. Fill the bag with the remaining meringue to make more cookies. Bake, without opening oven, for 1 hour. Reduce the oven temperature to 175° F and bake until meringues are completely dry—about 2 hours. Cool the meringues on the parchment paper or wire racks.

286. Caramel Thumbprints

Thumbprints, a classic Christmas cookie, are even more delicious when filled with buttery, creamy caramel. You can use a finger to make the indentation in the cookies, or use the end of the handle of a wooden spoon if you like.

Makes about 4 dozen cookies

3 cups all-purpose flour

2 teaspoons baking powder

$\frac{1}{2}$ teaspoon salt

$\frac{1}{2}$ cup plus 4 tablespoons unsalted butter (1$\frac{1}{2}$ sticks), softened

1$\frac{1}{2}$ cups firmly packed light brown sugar

2 large eggs

1 cup almond butter

1 teaspoon vanilla extract

$\frac{1}{2}$ teaspoon almond extract

$\frac{1}{2}$ cup sliced almonds, finely chopped

1 cup granulated sugar

$\frac{1}{4}$ cup water

2 tablespoons honey

$\frac{1}{4}$ cup heavy cream

1. Make the dough: Sift the flour, baking powder, and salt together into a medium bowl. Set aside. Beat $\frac{1}{2}$ cup plus 2 tablespoons butter in a large bowl using a mixer set on medium speed until creamy. Gradually add the brown sugar, and continue to beat until the sugar is incorporated. Add the eggs, one at a time, beating well after each addition. Add the almond butter and vanilla and almond extracts and beat thoroughly. Reduce the mixer speed to low and add the flour mixture, beating until a dough forms. Wrap the dough in plastic wrap and chill for 1 hour.

2. Bake the cookies: Preheat the oven to 350°F. Line two baking pans with parchment paper. Set aside. Put the almonds into a shallow dish. Set aside. Meanwhile, let the dough come to room temperature. Shape 1½-teaspoonfuls of the dough into balls. Roll the balls in the almonds to coat. Place, about 1 inch apart, on the prepared baking sheets, and press an indentation into the center of each ball. Chill for 10 minutes. Bake the cookies for 8 minutes. Remove the cookies from the oven and indent the cookies again. Continue to bake until lightly browned and firm—about 8 more minutes. Transfer the cookies to wire racks to cool completely.

3. Make the caramel centers: Combine the granulated sugar, water, and honey in a heavy medium saucepan. Cook over high heat until it reaches a dark amber color—about 12 minutes. Stir in remaining butter and the cream. Remove from the heat and cool. Spoon about 1 teaspoon soft caramel into the center of each cookie. Store in an airtight container for up to 1 week.

287. Mini Thumbprints with Currant Jam

This festive cookie recipe is a variation of the recipe for Caramel Thumbprints on page 190.

Makes about 10 dozen cookies

Make ½ recipe of the Caramel Thumbprints dough (see page 190), omitting the almond butter and almond extract. Form ½ teaspoonfuls of the dough into balls and roll in ½ cup turbinado instead of the almonds. Bake as directed, reducing the total baking time to 8 minutes (two 4-minute intervals). Instead of the caramel centers, fill the cooled cookies with ½ cup strained currant or strawberry preserves.

288. Holiday Cookie Cards

This holiday season, send cookie greeting cards packed in decorative, durable boxes that can remain a keepsake long after the cookies have been savored.

Makes 8 cookies

4 large egg whites

1 cup sugar

1 cup all-purpose flour

½ cup unsalted butter (1 stick), melted and cooled

1½ teaspoons ground aniseed

½ teaspoon vanilla extract

1. Make the batter: Whisk the egg whites and sugar together in a medium bowl until combined. Add the remaining flour, butter, aniseed, and vanilla and whisk until smooth. Cover with plastic wrap and chill for 1 to 24 hours.

2. Bake the cookies: Preheat the oven to 350°F. Cut out eight 10- by ½-inch-wide strips of paper, write your desired holiday messages on them, and set aside. On a nonstick baking sheet or baking sheet lined with a nonstick silicone mat, spread 3 tablespoons batter into an 8-inch round. Bake until lightly browned—about 7 minutes. Cool slightly, but make sure the cookie remains warm and pliable. Use a spatula to lift the cookie from the pan and turn it over. Place a prepared message strip in the center of the cookie and fold the cookie in half to form a loose semicircle. Do not flatten or crease the fold. Bend the 2 ends of the straight edge of the cookie in towards each other. Hold the cookie in this position until set, then transfer to a wire rack to cool completely. Repeat with the remaining batter. Store in an airtight container for up to 3 days.

289. Spritz Cookies

Buttery spritz cookies are a holiday classic. Half the fun when making them is choosing which cookie template to press the cookies through.

Makes about 6 dozen cookies

2 cups all-purpose flour

¼ teaspoon baking powder

¼ teaspoon salt

1 cup unsalted butter (2 sticks), softened

½ cup sugar

2 large egg yolks

2 teaspoons vanilla extract

2 teaspoons grated lemon zest

1. Make the dough: Sift the flour, baking powder, and salt together into a medium bowl. Set aside. Beat the butter in a large bowl with a mixer set on medium speed until creamy. Add the sugar in a slow stream and continue beating until incorporated. Add the yolks, vanilla, and lemon zest and beat thoroughly. Reduce the mixer speed to medium-low and add the flour mixture, beating until a smooth and pliable dough forms. Wrap the dough in plastic wrap and chill for 30 minutes.

2. Bake the cookies: Preheat the oven to 350°F. Following manufacturer's instructions, fill the cookie press with the dough and fit the press with a decorative template. Press the cookies, 1 inch apart, onto an ungreased baking sheet. Bake until the edges are browned—10 to 12 minutes. Transfer the cookies to wire racks to cool completely. Repeat with the remaining dough to make more cookies. Store in an airtight container for up to 1 week.

290. Pistachio-Cranberry Stacks

Package these playful striped cookies in vellum or other translucent paper envelopes for party favors and tie with ribbon. Their stripes will show through the envelopes, adding an additional visual element to the presentation. If you can't find cranberry preserve, use raspberry or strawberry instead.

Makes about 3 dozen cookies

1½ cups all-purpose flour

½ cup fine-ground yellow cornmeal

½ cup unsalted shelled pistachios, finely ground

½ teaspoon salt

½ cup unsalted butter (1 stick), softened

½ cup sugar

1 large egg

2 large egg yolks

1 teaspoon vanilla extract

2 cups dried cranberries

½ cup strained cranberry preserves

1. Make the dough: Combine the flour, cornmeal, pistachios, and salt in a medium bowl. Set aside. Beat the butter and sugar in a large bowl using a mixer set on medium speed until light and fluffy. Add the egg and egg yolks, one at a time, beating well after each addition, until thoroughly combined. Add the vanilla extract. Reduce the mixer speed to low, add the flour mixture, and beat until well combined. Shape the dough into a square, wrap in plastic wrap, and chill for 1 hour.

2. Make the filling: Place the cranberries in the bowl of a food processor fitted with a metal blade and process until finely chopped. Transfer the cranberries to a bowl and stir in the preserves.

3. Shape the cookies: On a lightly floured surface, roll the dough into a 10- by 10-inch square. Cut the dough into 5- by 2-inch strips and chill until firm. Spread a thin, even layer of the filling (about 2 tablespoons) over a strip of dough. Top with a second strip of dough and spread with more filling. Repeat until 4 layers of filling are sandwiched by 5 layers of dough. Trim the edges if necessary, wrap in plastic wrap, and freeze until solid—about 1 hour.

4. Bake the cookies: Preheat the oven to 350°F. Line 2 baking sheets with parchment paper. Slice the log crosswise into ¼-inch-thick cookies and place 2 inches apart on the prepared baking sheets. Bake until golden brown—13 to 15 minutes. Transfer the cookies to wire racks to cool completely. Store in an airtight container for up to 1 week.

291. Holiday Blondies

Simple ingredients applied with a bit of imagination ensure that these cookies are up to the occasion: puffed cereal sweetened with caramel turns this everyday blondie into a memorable treat worthy of gift giving.

Makes 16 squares

1 cup all-purpose flour

1/2 teaspoon baking powder

1/2 teaspoon salt

1 cup firmly packed light brown sugar

6 tablespoons unsalted butter (3/4 stick),
  melted and cooled slightly

1 large egg

2 large egg yolks

2 teaspoons vanilla extract

6 tablespoons chocolate-hazelnut spread,
  such as Nutella

3 1/2 cups Kix brand cereal

1 cup granulated sugar

1/4 cup water

1/4 teaspoon fresh lemon juice

1. Make the cookie crust: Preheat the oven to 350°F. Line the bottom of a 10-inch-square pan with parchment paper. Set aside. Sift the flour, baking powder, and salt together into a medium bowl. Set aside. Whisk the brown sugar, butter, egg, egg yolks, and vanilla together in a medium bowl. Add to the flour mixture and mix until combined well. Spread the dough in the bottom of the prepared pan. Bake until the edges are lightly browned—about 13 minutes. Cool in the pan on a wire rack for 15 minutes. Invert onto the wire rack, lift off the pan, and cool completely.

2. Assemble the cookies: Spread the chocolate-hazelnut spread over the crust and cut into 16 squares. Place the cereal in a large bowl. Set aside. Fill a large bowl with ice water. Set aside. Combine the granulated sugar, water, and lemon juice in a heavy small saucepan and cook over high heat until it turns a light amber color—about 10 minutes. Dip the bottom of the pan into the ice water to stop the cooking, then pour 6 to 8 tablespoons of the caramel onto the cereal. Toss until well coated, adding more caramel if necessary. Working quickly, form the cereal into small clusters and place on the blondie squares. Drizzle with the remaining caramel and cool completely. Store, in a single layer, in an airtight container for up to 5 days.

292. Sugar-Cookie Stars

Dangle these sugar-cookie stars from miniature trees and invite visitors to help themselves.

Makes about 6 dozen cookies

5 cups all-purpose flour

2 teaspoons ground nutmeg

$\frac{1}{2}$ teaspoon salt

2 cups unsalted butter (4 sticks), softened

1$\frac{1}{4}$ cups sugar

2 large eggs

3 large egg yolks

2 teaspoons vanilla extract

2 tablespoons grated orange zest

1 tablespoon heavy cream

1. Make the dough: Sift the flour, nutmeg, and salt together into a medium bowl. Set aside. Beat the butter in a large bowl, using a mixer set on medium speed, until creamy. Add the sugar in a steady stream and continue to beat until incorporated. Add the eggs, 2 of the egg yolks, the vanilla, and orange zest and beat thoroughly. Reduce the mixer speed to medium-low, add the flour mixture, and beat until combined. Divide the dough in half, shape each piece into a 6- by 4-inch rectangle, and wrap in plastic wrap. Chill for 4 to 24 hours.

2. Cut out the cookies: Preheat the oven to 350°F. Line 2 baking sheets with parchment paper. Set aside. On a lightly floured surface, roll out the dough to $\frac{1}{8}$-inch thickness. Using cookie cutters of your choice, cut out shapes and place them 2 inches apart on the prepared baking sheets. If you wish to hang the cookies, prick the tops with the blunt end of a wooden skewer to create holes. Gather up the dough scraps, form into a disk, and rechill. Repeat to make more cookies.

3. Bake the cookies: Beat the remaining egg yolk and the cream in a small bowl. Brush the cookies very lightly with the egg wash. Bake, rotating the pans halfway through, until the cookies are golden brown—about 15 minutes. If you made holes, prick the cookies again when you rotate the pans to keep the holes open. Transfer the cookies to wire racks to cool completely. Store in an airtight container for up to 1 week.

293. Double-Chocolate Snowquakes

It just isn't the holidays without cookies! A generous coating of confectioners' sugar covers rich chocolate cookie balls which crack and puff up when baked. (See photo on page 174.)

Makes 4 dozen cookies

1½ cups all-purpose flour

¾ cup Dutch-processed unsweetened cocoa

2 teaspoons baking powder

¾ teaspoon salt

½ cup unsalted butter (1 stick), softened

¾ cup firmly packed dark brown sugar

¼ cup granulated sugar

2 large eggs

1 teaspoon vanilla extract

1¼ cups milk-chocolate chips

1 cup confectioners' sugar

1. Make the dough: Combine the flour, cocoa, baking powder, and salt in a medium bowl and set aside. Beat the butter in a large bowl using an electric mixer set on medium speed until creamy. Add the sugars and beat until incorporated. Add the eggs and vanilla and beat thoroughly. Reduce the mixer speed to medium low, add the flour mixture, and beat until a soft dough forms. Stir in the chocolate chips. Cover the dough with plastic wrap and chill for 1 hour.

2. Bake the cookies: Preheat the oven to 350°F. Line 2 baking sheets with parchment paper. Set aside. Place the confectioners' sugar in a medium bowl. Set aside. Roll the dough in balls using 1 tablespoonful of dough for each ball. Roll the balls in the confectioners' sugar to coat generously—do not shake off the excess sugar. Place the balls, 2 inches apart, on the prepared baking sheets. Bake until puffed, cracked, and slightly firm to the touch—10 to 12 minutes. Transfer the cookies to wire racks to cool completely. Store in an airtight container for up to 1 week.

294. Coffee-Cream Sandwiches

With a little imagination, the season's sweet lineup can leave a lasting impression. The key is to present cookies in the most memorable ways. For example, tie them up with pretty ribbon into appetizing little bundles, as we did, to hand out as party favors.

Makes about 4 dozen cookies

1 large egg

$\frac{2}{3}$ cup all-purpose flour

$\frac{1}{3}$ cup sugar

$2\frac{1}{2}$ tablespoons unsalted butter, melted and cooled

$\frac{3}{4}$ teaspoon baking powder

$\frac{1}{2}$ teaspoon pure vanilla extract

2 tablespoons instant espresso powder

2 teaspoons boiling water

$\frac{1}{2}$ cup unsalted butter (1 stick), softened

2 cups confectioners' sugar, sifted

$\frac{1}{2}$ cup plus 2 tablespoons mascarpone

1. Make the cookies: Combine the egg, flour, sugar, butter, baking powder, and vanilla in a medium bowl. Beat using a mixer set on low speed until smooth—about 1 minute. Following the manufacturer's instructions, make the cookies in a preheated pizzelle iron: Using a generous $\frac{1}{4}$ teaspoonful of batter per cookie, cook for 45 seconds to 1 minute. (Be careful: Unwatched batter will burn quickly.) Lift the cookie from the iron and transfer to a wire rack to cool completely. Repeat with the remaining batter.

2. Make the filling: Dissolve the espresso powder in the water and let cool. Using a mixer set on medium speed, cream the softened butter in a medium bowl until smooth. Add the confectioners' sugar and continue to beat until fluffy. Add espresso mixture and beat to incorporate. Stir in the mascarpone.

3. Assemble the cookies: Place 2 teaspoonfuls filling between 2 cookies. Repeat with the remaining filling and cookies. Store in an airtight container for up to 3 days.

Delight your loved ones with an offering of cake.

295. Brown-Sugar Pound Cake

Send guests home with a sweet memory: let them tuck a miniature, cellophane-wrapped Brown-Sugar Pound Cake into their coat pockets as they say their thanks.

Makes 16 Servings (Four 5- by 2-inch cakes)

3 cups cake flour

½ teaspoon salt

¼ teaspoon baking soda

¼ teaspoon ground nutmeg

1½ cups unsalted butter (3 sticks), softened

1½ cups firmly packed dark brown sugar

½ cup granulated sugar

5 large eggs

1 teaspoon vanilla extract

½ cup buttermilk

1. Make the batter: Preheat the oven to 350°F. Lightly coat four 5- by 2½-inch miniature loaf pans with vegetable-oil cooking spray. Set aside. Sift the flour, salt, baking soda, and nutmeg together into a medium bowl. Beat the butter and sugars in a large bowl using a mixer set on high speed until light and fluffy—about 5 minutes. Add the eggs, one at a time, beating well after each addition. Add the vanilla. Reduce the mixer speed to low and add the flour mixture by thirds, alternating with the buttermilk and ending with the dry ingredients, mixing just until the batter is smooth.

2. Bake the cake: Divide the batter equally among the prepared pans and bake until a tester inserted into the center of each cake comes out clean—40 to 50 minutes. Cool in the pans on wire racks for 10 minutes. Use a knife to loosen the cakes from the sides of the pans and invert onto the wire racks to cool completely.

296. Coconut Cake

This elegant cake features a luscious coconut custard that is spread between each layer. The cake needs to be prepared at least ten hours ahead to allow enough time for the custard to set.

Makes 16 servings (one 9-inch cake)

1½ cups cake flour

½ teaspoon baking powder

¼ teaspoon salt

5 large eggs, separated

½ cup cold water

2 cups plus 1 tablespoon sugar

2 teaspoons vanilla extract

¼ cup dark rum

1 cup water

1½ cups heavy cream

1½ cups sweetened flaked coconut, toasted

Coconut Custard (recipe follows)

1. Make the cake: Preheat the oven to 350°F. Lightly butter a 9- by 3-inch springform pan. Line the bottom of the pan with parchment paper. Butter the parchment and dust with flour. Tap out any excess. Set aside. Sift the flour, baking powder, and salt together into a large bowl. Set aside. Beat the egg yolks and water together in a medium bowl using an electric mixer set on

medium for 1 minute. Gradually add 1½ cups sugar. Add 1 teaspoon vanilla extract. Increase the mixer speed to high and beat until thick and pale— about 4 minutes. Beat the egg whites with clean beaters in a large bowl using a mixer set on high speed until soft peaks form—about 2 minutes. Sift the flour mixture over the egg-yolk mixture and fold to combine. Fold in the egg whites: Pour the batter into the prepared pan and bake until a toothpick inserted into the center of the cake comes out clean—about 45 minutes. Avoid opening the oven door for the first 30 minutes. Cool in the pan on a wire rack. Release the sides of the pan.

2. Assemble the cake: Bring ½ cup sugar, rum, and water to a boil in a small saucepan over high heat. Cook, stirring occasionally, for 5 minutes. Remove from the heat. Use a serrated knife to split the cake into 3 layers. Brush each layer generously with the rum syrup. Place the bottom layer on a serving plate and top with half of the custard. Repeat with the next layer and remaining custard. Top with the remaining layer. Brush the cake with remaining syrup, cover with plastic wrap, and refrigerate for at least 10 hours or up to 24.

3. Prepare the whipped-cream frosting: Beat the cream, remaining vanilla, and remaining sugar in a large bowl until soft peaks form. Spread the cream evenly over the top and sides of the cake. Sprinkle the toasted coconut over the top and gently press it onto the sides. Chill for up to 2 hours.

Coconut Custard

3 tablespoons all-purpose flour

1½ cups milk

½ cup sugar

1 vanilla bean, seeds scraped, pod reserved

5 large egg yolks

1 cup sweetened flaked coconut

Make the custard: Whisk the flour and ½ cup milk together in a small bowl. Combine the remaining milk, the sugar, and vanilla bean seeds and pod in a small saucepan over medium-low heat. Cook, stirring, until the sugar is dissolved. Whisk in the flour mixture and cook until thickened—about 3 minutes. Whisk the egg yolks together in a large bowl. Slowly add half the hot-milk mixture to the egg yolks, whisking constantly. Return the mixture to the saucepan. Cook, stirring constantly, over medium heat until mixture begins to bubble and thicken—about 3 minutes. Strain through a fine sieve into a bowl and fold in the coconut. Cool completely. Store refrigerated in an airtight container until ready to use.

297. Chocolate Espresso Torte

A classic combination of chocolate and espresso, this elegant chocolate cake, glazed with decadent ganache, is the perfect finale to a special holiday meal.

Makes 12 servings (one 9- by 9-inch cake)

21 ounces semisweet chocolate, chopped

1½ cups unsalted butter (3 sticks), softened

2 tablespoons instant espresso powder or coffee crystals

5 large eggs, separated, at room temperature

¾ cup sugar

½ cup all-purpose flour

¼ teaspoon salt

1 tablespoon vanilla extract

½ teaspoon cream of tartar

2 tablespoons heavy cream

1 tablespoon light corn syrup

1. Make the batter: Preheat the oven to 350°F. Butter a 9-inch square pan. Line the bottom with parchment paper and butter the paper. Set aside. Melt 9 ounces of chocolate, ¾ cup butter, and the espresso powder in a double boiler set over low heat. Remove from the heat. Beat the egg yolks in a large bowl using a mixer set on medium speed, until foamy—15 to 30 seconds. Add ½ cup sugar and continue to beat until thick and pale—about 3 minutes. Reduce the mixer speed to low and add the chocolate mixture, flour, salt, and vanilla. Set aside. Combine the egg whites and cream of tartar in a medium bowl. With clean beaters, beat on medium speed until soft peaks form. Add the remaining sugar in a steady stream and beat until stiff, glossy peaks form. Fold the beaten whites into the chocolate mixture, one third at a time, until incorporated.

2. Bake the cake: Pour the batter into the prepared pan and bake until a tester inserted into the center of the cake comes out clean—about 35 minutes. Cool in the pan on a wire rack for 30 minutes. Invert the cake onto a wire rack and peel off the parchment paper. Cool completely.

3. Make the ganache glaze: Melt the remaining 12 ounces chocolate in a double boiler set over low heat. Remove from the heat and stir in the remaining butter until combined. Stir in the cream and corn syrup. Allow the glaze to cool until thick enough to coat yet still pours easily— 2 to 3 minutes. Set the cake on the wire rack on a piece of waxed paper. Pour the glaze onto the center of the cake and use a narrow metal spatula to smooth it evenly over the top and sides. Let the cake sit until the glaze sets—about 10 minutes. Using 1 or 2 wide spatulas as an aid, carefully transfer the cake to a serving plate.

298. Spiced Gingerbread Cake

The heady aroma of gingerbread cake signals the arrival of the holidays. A potent mix of ginger, cloves, cinnamon, and other winter spices, it's a traditional favorite.

Makes 12 servings (one 9-inch cake)

2½ cups all-purpose flour

4 teaspoons ground ginger

2 teaspoons baking soda

2 teaspoons ground cinnamon

1 teaspoon ground allspice

1 teaspoon ground nutmeg

½ teaspoon ground cloves

½ teaspoon salt

½ cup unsalted butter (1 stick), softened

½ cup firmly packed light brown sugar

2 large eggs

1 teaspoon grated orange zest

1 cup boiling water

¾ cup dark molasses

¼ cup orange juice

1. Make the batter: Preheat the oven to 350°F. Lightly coat a 9-inch square pan with butter or vegetable-oil cooking spray. Dust with flour and tap out any excess. Set aside. Combine the flour, ginger, baking soda, cinnamon, allspice, nutmeg, cloves, and salt in a large bowl. Set aside. Beat butter in a large bowl using an electric mixer set on medium-high speed for 3 minutes. Add the brown sugar and continue to beat until light and fluffy—about 3 more minutes. Reduce the mixer speed to low and add the eggs, one at a time, beating well after each addition. Mix in the orange zest. Set aside. Combine the boiling water, molasses, and orange juice in a large glass measuring cup. Set aside. With mixer on low speed, add the flour mixture by thirds, alternating with the molasses mixture and ending with the dry ingredients, mixing just until the batter is smooth.

2. Bake the cake: Pour the batter into the prepared cake pan and bake until a toothpick inserted into the center of the cake comes out clean—about 45 minutes. Cool in the pan on a wire rack for 5 minutes. Remove the cake from pan and place on a wire rack to cool completely.

A golden touch: To turn a homey gingerbread cake into an elegant finale to a holiday meal, add a glimmering gold leaf accent. While the cake is still warm, take a single sheet of edible gold leaf and lightly press, leaf-side down, onto the cake's surface, rubbing gently over the back of the leaf. Peel off the backing paper. Use an entire sheet to make a gilded diamond, or before applying, cut the gold leaf into a holiday design (make a cardboard version first to use as a guide). If you don't have the time to try gilding, decorate with edible glitter, dust with luster dust, or use a few silvery dragées.

299. Four-Layer Gingerbread Cake

Moist and subtly spiced, this cake is neatly "wrapped" in white-chocolate buttercream and "tied" with chocolate ribbon. If you make the layers in advance and freeze them, on the day of the party all you'll have to do is whip up the buttercream and frost the cake.

Makes 24 servings (One 9-inch 4-layer cake)

5 cups all-purpose flour

5 teaspoons ground ginger

4 teaspoons baking soda

2 teaspoons ground cinnamon

1 teaspoon ground allspice

1 teaspoon ground nutmeg

1 teaspoon salt

$\frac{1}{2}$ teaspoon ground cloves

2 cups boiling water

1 12-ounce jar dark molasses

$\frac{1}{2}$ cup orange juice

1 cup unsalted butter (2 sticks), softened

1 cup firmly packed light brown sugar

4 large eggs

2 teaspoons grated orange zest

White-Chocolate Buttercream (recipe follows)

Chocolate Ribbon (recipe follows)

1. Make the batter: Preheat the oven to 350°F. Lightly coat four 9-inch square pans with vegetable-oil cooking spray and set aside. Combine the flour, ginger, baking soda, cinnamon, allspice, nutmeg, salt, and cloves in a large bowl. Set aside. Combine the boiling water, molasses, and orange juice in a 4-cup glass measuring cup or medium bowl. Set aside. Cream the butter in a large bowl with a mixer set on medium-high speed for 3 minutes. Add the brown sugar and continue to beat until light and fluffy—about 3 more minutes. Reduce the mixer speed to low and add the eggs, one at a time, beating well after each addition. Beat in the orange zest. Add the flour mixture by thirds, alternating with the molasses mixture and ending with the dry ingredients, mixing until the batter is smooth.

2. Bake the cake: Divide the batter equally among the prepared pans and bake until a tester inserted into the center of each cake layer comes out clean—20 to 25 minutes. Cool in the pans on wire racks for 5 minutes. Use a knife to loosen the cake layers from the sides of the pans and invert onto the wire racks to cool completely.

3. Assemble the cake: Line the edges of a cake plate with 3-inch-wide strips of waxed or parchment paper and place a cake layer on top. Place $\frac{2}{3}$ cup of White-Chocolate Buttercream on top of the layer and spread evenly. Repeat with 2 more cake layers. Place the fourth cake layer on top and spread a thin layer of buttercream over the

baking

★

211

assembled layers to seal in the crumbs. Chill for 20 minutes. Use the remaining buttercream to frost the top and sides of the cake. Place the chocolate ribbon on the cake and refrigerate for up to 8 hours. Set the cake out at room temperature for 30 minutes before serving.

White-Chocolate Buttercream

3 cups water

12 large egg whites

$\frac{1}{2}$ cup granulated sugar

$2\frac{1}{4}$ cups unsalted butter ($4\frac{1}{2}$ sticks), softened

18 ounces white chocolate, melted and cooled

Make the buttercream: Bring the water to a boil in a 3-quart saucepan and reduce the heat to maintain a slow simmer. Combine the egg whites and sugar in a large bowl and set over the simmering water, making sure the bottom of the bowl does not touch the water. Whisk by hand or with a hand mixer set on low speed until the sugar dissolves and the mixture is very hot to the touch—7 to 10 minutes. Remove the bowl from heat and beat on high speed until the whites are glossy and thoroughly cooled—7 to 10 more minutes. Add the butter to the beaten whites, 2 tablespoons at a time, and beat just until incorporated. As the butter is added, the frosting may appear curdled. The frosting will become smooth and glossy as it continues to be beaten. Gradually add the white chocolate and beat until the frosting is fluffy—about 5 more minutes.

Chocolate Ribbon

3 cups water

4 ounces semisweet chocolate, chopped

3 tablespoons light corn syrup

1 tablespoon unsweetened cocoa for sprinkling onto work surface

1. Prepare the chocolate: Bring the water to a boil in a 3-quart saucepan and reduce the heat to maintain a slow simmer. Place the chocolate in a medium bowl and set over the simmering water, making sure the bottom of the bowl does not touch the water. Stir the chocolate until it melts, then remove from the heat.

2. Make the chocolate ribbon: Stir the corn syrup into the melted chocolate until the mixture is thoroughly blended and forms a soft ball. Wrap in plastic wrap and let stand at room temperature until the mixture reaches the consistency of modeling clay—about 30 minutes. (If preparing a day ahead, wrap tightly in plastic wrap and store at room temperature. To use, knead the still-wrapped dough until pliable.)

3. Form the ribbon: Remove the plastic wrap and sprinkle the work surface with the cocoa. Roll out the chocolate modeling ribbon into a narrow rectangle $\frac{1}{4}$ to $\frac{1}{8}$ inch thick. With a pastry wheel or tip of a sharp knife, cut 2 strips of ribbon, each about 13 inches long and 1 inch wide. Cut a "V" into each end of the ribbon. Crisscross the strips of ribbon over the cake to resemble a gift package.

300. Gingerbread House

Homemade gingerbread houses lend an extra measure of holiday magic to your home. The fun begins with the process of mixing the spiced dough and making the colorful icings before "building" the structure and, finally, decorating the architectural confection as simply or elaborately as your heart desires. By using the gingerbread and royal icing recipes and the step-by-step instructions on the following pages, you can build a gingerbread dream house—or an entire village. Before you start, read through the instructions, gather all the materials, and form a plan with manageable segments. For example, make and bake the dough one day and create the stained-glass windows the next. Assemble on yet another day, and decorate later.

Here's what you'll need to get started: 1 set of baked gingerbread-house pieces (2 sides; 1 front; 1 back; and 2 roofs—see recipe below), 20 multicolored hard candies (such as Lifesavers or sourballs); one 10-inch-diameter, heavy-gauge cardboard circle; red, green, and white royal icing (see recipe below); 3 pastry bags; 3 pastry tips (a plain round—about $1/16$-inch opening; a small open star tip—about $1/8$-inch opening; and a medium open star tip—about $1/4$-inch opening; or professional tips, sizes #3, #16, and #21); coarse, white sugar crystals; 4 miniature candy canes; 1 battery-operated light, small enough to fit through a 2-inch opening and no taller than 8 inches.

Gingerbread

Before you begin, enlarge the template on page 217 and transfer to medium-gauge cardboard or foam core. Wiped clean after using and stored in a dry place, the templates will last for years and may be used over and over. Leftover dough scraps can be used to make miniature gingerbread people to decorate your house or Christmas tree.

Makes 1 gingerbread house

1½ cups vegetable shortening

1½ cups sugar

1 tablespoon ground cinnamon

2 teaspoons ground ginger

1 teaspoon ground cloves

1 teaspoon ground nutmeg

1 teaspoon salt

1 teaspoon vanilla extract

12-ounce jar dark molasses

6½ cups all-purpose flour

1. Make the dough: Beat the vegetable shortening and sugar in a large bowl using a mixer set on medium speed until well blended—1 to 1½ minutes. Add the cinnamon, ginger, cloves, nutmeg, and salt and continue to beat until incorporated. Add the vanilla and molasses and beat for 30 more seconds. If using a stand mixer, add the flour 1 cup at a time. Otherwise, stir in the flour using a wooden spoon, kneading in the final cups of flour by hand. Divide the dough in half and shape each piece into 1½-inch-thick squares. Wrap in plastic wrap. Set aside.

2. Cut out shapes: Preheat the oven to 350°F. Between 2 sheets of waxed or parchment paper, roll each dough half into a 16- by 12-inch rectangle, about ¼ inch thick. Lightly coat 1 roof, side, and front template with vegetable-oil nonstick cooking spray and position them on one piece of the dough. Cut out the outlines and windows of the templates, and remove any excess dough. Set aside. Repeat the process, to cut out 1 roof, side, and back template.

3. Bake the gingerbread: Carefully slide a rimless baking sheet under the parchment of each set of cut-out dough pieces. Make sure that the dough is completely flat and bake until the gingerbread is firm but not hard to the touch—20 to 25 minutes. Cool on the baking sheets on wire racks for 10 minutes. Transfer the dough pieces on the parchment paper to wire racks to cool completely.

Royal Icing

Makes enough icing for one house.

2 pounds confectioners' sugar

4 large egg whites

Red and green professional-strength liquid-paste food colors

1. Beat the confectioners' sugar and egg whites in a large bowl using a mixer set on at medium speed until well blended. The resulting icing should be smooth, glossy, and able to hold a distinct shape. Place 1 cup of icing in each of 2 small bowls. Add 2 or 3 drops of red color to one bowl of icing and 2 or 3 drops of green to the other. Mix well to achieve a uniform color. Transfer the remaining white icing to a third bowl. Cover all the bowls tightly with plastic wrap. Set aside.

Note: Because this recipe contains raw eggs, the icing should not be eaten. To make icing safe for consumption, use meringue powder and follow the package instructions to make edible Royal Icing.

Gingerbread-House Construction Tips

Stained-Glass Window and Door:

1. Preheat the oven to 350° F. Place the baked gingerbread house sides, front, and back on a parchment paper or foil-lined baking sheet. Put the hard candies in a food processor fitted with the metal blade and pulse to grind to a powder. Fill all of the window spaces with the ground candy and bake until the powder melts into smooth translucent panes—4 to 5 minutes. Let cool completely on the baking sheets on wire racks, then transfer to wire racks.

2. Fill a pastry bag fitted with a small round pastry tip with white royal icing. Pipe windowpanes, shutters, and a door. Set aside to dry—about 30 minutes.

Assemble the house:

1. Cut a 2-inch hole in the cardboard circle and set aside. Change the round tip to the medium star tip. Pipe a line of icing along one edge of the front piece of the gingerbread house. Do not pipe along slanted roof edge. Stand the front piece $1\frac{1}{2}$ inches from the edge of the cardboard circle base. Fit a side piece against the edge of the front piece. Hold until the two pieces adhere. Repeat for the second side. Pipe icing along the inside side edges of the back piece of the house and fit it against the two open sides. Adjust the alignment and let the icing set for 30 minutes. Pipe along the slanted edges and set the

roof pieces on top of the structure. Allow to set until completely dry or overnight.

Decorate the house:

1. Fit a pastry bag with a small star tip and fill with green icing. Form bushes, a wreath, and trees by piping clusters of tiny rosettes.

2. Fit a pastry bag with a small round tip and fill it with red icing. Pipe tiny dots of icing to mimic berries on the bushes, wreath, and trees. Change to a medium star tip and pipe decorative swirls down the house corners and slanted roof edges to cover the white adhesive icing.

3. Using a small offset or icing spatula, spread white icing over one side of the roof, "dripping" some of the icing along the bottom edge to create icicles. Sprinkle with sugar crystals. Repeat for the other side. Pipe a straight line along the roof's peak and attach the candy canes. Using the spatula, spread more of the white icing over the entire base to create snow and drifts.

4. Allow to dry overnight. Insert the light through the hole in the cardboard base and display lit house.

Icing advice: Royal icing serves as both adornment and glue for this house. Work as quickly as possible, as the icing dries fast. To prevent drying, cover the bowl; a few drops of water will restore its texture. Practice piping designs on parchment paper to perfect your technique.

When "gluing" the house pieces together, hold the pieces together with your hands until the pieces are secure.

Builder's notes: Gingerbread-house building is a great group project. Children will definitely want to join in, so assign young "construction" workers tasks according to age. Older children can trace and cut out the templates and dough and provide an extra pair of hands during assembly. (If you don't have any additional help during assembly, try using a heavy can as a support on the inside of the house. Just remember to remove it before the roof is attached.) Younger children can help roll the dough out and will enjoy icing the roof and base of the house. With a little organization, this project will be as fun as it's meant to be.

Decorating note: Although this house is decorated quite simply—with a piped-on evergreen wreath, shrubs, and window boxes—individual inspiration can transform any house into a grand palace. Use your imagination to add distinctive ornaments, such as dried fruits, flaked coconut, pretzel sticks, and cereal.

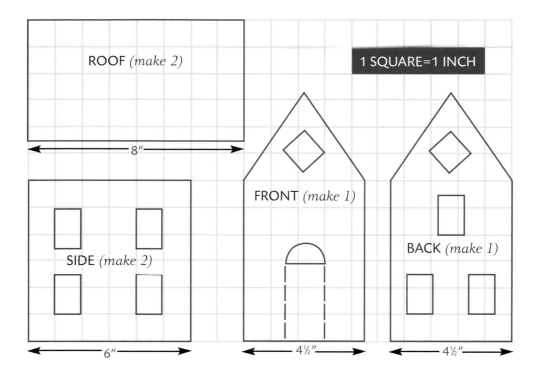

ROOF (make 2)

1 SQUARE=1 INCH

8"

FRONT (make 1)

SIDE (make 2)

BACK (make 1)

6"

4½"

4½"

301. Enter your dream gingerbread house in the National Gingerbread House Competition in Asheville, North Carolina, which was started in 1993. Entries are judged on their overall appearance, originality, degree of difficulty, precision, and consistency of theme. And every element of the house—from the landscape shrubbery to the rooftop finial—must be completely edible. For details and a contest entry form go to www.groveparkinn.com or call 828-252-2711 ext. 8045.

Photography Credits

Page 1: Andrew McCaul
Page 2: Keith Scott Morton
Page 3: Steven Randazzo
Page 4 (top left): Andrew McCaul
Page 4 (middle left): Kindra Clineff
Page 4 (bottom left):
Page 4 (right): Toshi Otsuki
Page 6: David Prince
Page 8: Kindra Clineff
Idea no. 1: David Prince
Idea no. 3: Susie Cushner
Idea no. 4: Robin Stubbert
Idea no. 5: Keith Scott Morton
Idea no. 6: Toshi Otsuki
Idea no. 7: Gridley & Graves
Idea no. 8: Toshi Otsuki
Idea no. 9: William P. Steele
Idea no. 11: Keith Scott Morton
Idea no. 12: Keith Scott Morton
Idea no. 13: Steven Randazzo
Idea no. 14: Steven Randazzo
Idea no. 16: Keith Scott Morton
Idea no. 17: Jim Bastardo
Idea no. 18: Keith Scott Morton
Idea no. 19: Keith Scott Morton
Idea no. 21: Robin Stubbert
Idea no. 22: Kindra Clineff
Idea no. 23: Keith Scott Morton
Idea no. 24: Charles Schiller
Idea no. 25: Robin Stubbert
Idea no. 27: Kindra Clineff
Idea no. 28: Andrew McCaul
Idea no. 30: Toshi Otsuki
Idea no. 31: Michael Luppino
Idea no. 33: Keith Scott Morton
Idea no. 34: Steven Randazzo
Idea no. 36: John Blais
Idea no. 37: Andrew McCaul
Idea no. 38: Keith Scott Morton
Idea no. 40: Steven Randazzo
Idea no. 41: Keith Scott Morton
Idea no. 42: Keith Scott Morton

Idea no. 43: Steven Randazzo
Idea no. 44: Keith Scott Morton
Idea no. 46: Franklin and Esther Schmidt
Idea no. 47: Steven Randazzo
Idea no. 48: Franklin and Esther Schmidt
Idea no. 49: Toshi Otsuki
Idea no. 50: Kindra Clineff
Idea no. 51: Christophe Dugied
Idea no. 52: Steven Randazzo
Idea no. 53: Kindra Clineff
Idea no. 56: Kindra Clineff
Idea no. 57: Kindra Clineff
Idea no. 58: Kindra Clineff
Idea no. 59: Keith Scott Morton
Idea no. 60: Steven Randazzo
Idea no. 61: Keith Scott Morton
Idea no. 62: Steven Randazzo
Idea no. 64: Grey Crawford
Idea no. 65: Kristen Strecker
Idea no. 66: Keith Scott Morton
Idea no. 67: Jim Bastardo
Idea no. 68: Robin Stubbert
Idea no. 69: David Montgomery
Idea no. 70: David Prince
Idea no. 71: Gridley & Graves
Idea no. 72: Michael Luppino
Idea no. 73: Gridley & Graves
Idea no. 74: Kindra Clineff
Idea no. 75: Charles Maraia
Idea no. 76: Robin Stubbert
Idea no. 77: Toshi Otsuki
Idea no. 78: Steven Randazzo
Idea no. 79: Steven Randazzo
Idea no. 80: Kindra Clineff
Idea no. 81: Kindra Clineff
Idea no. 82: Susan Gentry McWhinney
Idea no. 83: Robin Stubbert
Idea no. 84: Keith Scott Morton
Idea no. 86: Steven Randazzo
Idea no. 87: Tara Sgroi
Idea no. 88: William P. Steele
Idea no. 89: Richard W. Brown

Idea no. 90: Toshi Otsuki
Idea no. 91: William P. Steele
Idea no. 92: Keith Scott Morton
Idea no. 93: Robin Stubbert
Idea no. 94: Toshi Otsuki
Idea no. 95: Robin Stubbert
Idea no. 96: Keith Scott Morton
Idea no. 98: Grey Crawford
Idea no. 99: Grey Crawford
Idea no. 100: Steven Randazzo
Idea no. 101: Franklin and Esther Schmidt
Idea no. 102: Grey Crawford
Idea no. 103: Steven Randazzo
Idea no. 104: Keith Scott Morton
Idea no. 105: David Prince
Idea no. 107: Michael Luppino
Idea no. 108: Michael Luppino
Idea no. 110: Kindra Clineff
Idea no. 111: Susan McWhinney
Idea no. 112: Christian Petersen
Idea no. 113: Kindra Clineff
Idea no. 114: Kindra Clineff
Idea no. 115: Charles Schiller
Idea no. 117: Steven Randazzo
Idea no. 118: Keith Scott Morton
Idea no. 119: Steven Randazzo
Idea no. 120: Steven Randazzo
Idea no. 122: Charles Schiller
Idea no. 123: Steven Randazzo
Idea no. 124: John Blais
Idea no. 126: Keith Scott Morton
Idea no. 127: Steven Randazzo
Idea no. 128: David Montgomery
Idea no. 129: Kindra Clineff
Idea no. 131: Kindra Clineff
Idea no. 132: Kindra Clineff
Idea no. 133: William P. Steele
Idea no. 134: Brooke Slezak
Idea no. 136: Keith Scott Morton
Idea no. 137: Andrew McCaul
Idea no. 138: Keith Scott Morton
Idea no. 139: Kindra Clineff
Idea no. 140: Kindra Clineff
Idea no. 142: Thomas Petri
Idea no. 143: Keith Scott Morton
Idea no. 144: Keith Scott Morton
Idea no. 145: Robin Stubbert
Idea no. 146: Steven Randazzo
Idea no. 147: Steven Randazzo

Idea no. 149: John Blais
Idea no. 150: Kindra Clineff
Idea no. 151: Kindra Clineff
Idea no. 152: Grey Crawford
Idea no. 153: Kindra Clineff
Idea no. 154: Keith Scott Morton
Idea no. 156: Steven Randazzo
Idea no. 157: Steven Randazzo
Idea no. 159: Steven Randazzo
Idea no. 160: Keith Scott Morton
Idea no. 161: Kindra Clineff
Idea no. 162: Steven Randazzo
Idea no. 163: Kindra Clineff
Idea no. 164: Michael Luppino
Page 102: Luciana Pampalone
Idea no. 165: Kindra Clineff
Idea no. 166: Brooke Slezak
Idea no. 167: Keith Scott Morton
Idea no. 168: Maura McEvoy
Idea no. 169: William P. Steele
Idea no. 170: David Prince
Idea no. 171: Ann Stratton
Idea no. 173: Donna Griffith
Idea no. 174: David Prince
Idea no. 175: Christophe Dugied
Idea no. 176: David Prince
Idea no. 177: Steven Randazzo
Idea no. 178: Steven Randazzo
Idea no. 179: Keith Scott Morton
Idea no. 180: Christian Petersen
Idea no. 181: Steven Randazzo
Idea no. 182: Steven Randazzo
Idea no. 183: John Gruen
Idea no. 184: Brooke Slezak
Idea no. 185: Jeff McNamara
Idea no. 186: Susan McWhinney
Idea no. 187: Luciana Pampalone
Idea no. 188: Christopher Drake
Idea no. 189: Keith Scott Morton
Idea no. 190: John Gruen
Idea no. 191: Charles Maraia
Idea no. 192: Robin Stubbert
Idea no. 193: David Prince
Idea no. 195: Susan Gentry McWhinney
Idea no. 196: Keith Scott Morton
Idea no. 197: Keith Scott Morton
Idea no. 198: Charles Maraia
Idea no. 199: David Prince
Page 126: Steven Randazzo

Idea no. 200: Keith Scott Morton
Idea no. 201: John Blais
Idea no. 202: Keith Scott Morton
Idea no. 203: Keith Scott Morton
Idea no. 204: Keith Scott Morton
Idea no. 205: William P. Steele
Idea no. 206: Jim Bastardo
Idea no. 207: Susan Gentry McWhinney
Idea no. 208: Susan Gentry McWhinney
Idea no. 209: Toshi Otsuki
Idea no. 210: Keith Scott Morton
Idea no. 211: William P. Steele
Idea no. 212: Keith Scott Morton
Idea no. 213: Charles Maraia
Idea no. 214: Christina Schmidhofer
Idea no. 215: David Prince
Idea no. 216: Steven Randazzo
Idea no. 217: Steven Randazzo
Idea no. 218: Christopher Drake
Idea no. 219: Steven Randazzo
Idea no. 220: Steven Randazzo
Idea no. 221: Jim Bastardo
Idea no. 222: Jim Bastardo
Idea no. 224: Susan Gentry McWhinney
Idea no. 225: Robin Stubbert
Idea no. 227: Susie Cushner
Idea no. 228: Keller & Keller
Idea no. 229: Catherine Gratwicke
Idea no. 231: Michael Luppino
Idea no. 232: Steven Randazzo
Idea no. 233: Keith Scott Morton
Idea no. 234: Andrew McCaul
Idea no. 235: Keith Scott Morton
Idea no. 236: Keith Scott Morton
Idea no. 237: Susan McWhinney
Idea no. 238: Robin Stubbert
Idea no. 239: Toshi Otsuki
Idea no. 240: Steven Randazzo
Idea no. 241: Keith Scott Morton
Idea no. 242: Keith Scott Morton
Idea no. 243: Susan Gentry McWhinney
Idea no. 244: Steven Randazzo
Idea no. 245: Charles Schiller
Idea no. 246: Courtesy of *Country Living*
Idea no. 247: Steven Randazzo
Idea no. 248: Steven Randazzo

Idea no. 249: Steven Randazzo
Idea no. 250: Steven Randazzo
Idea no. 252: Susan Gentry McWhinney
Idea no. 253: Susan Gentry McWhinney
Idea no. 254: Steven Randazzo
Idea no. 255: Susan McWhinney
Idea no. 256: Susan Gentry McWhinney
Idea no. 257: John Bessler
Idea no. 258: Susan McWhinney
Idea no. 259: Philippe Kress
Idea no. 260: Philippe Kress
Page 166: Ann Stratton
Idea no. 261: Kindra Clineff
Idea no. 262: James Worrell
Idea no. 264: Andrew McCaul
Idea no. 266: Kindra Clineff
Idea no. 267: Kindra Clineff
Idea no. 268: Kindra Clineff
Idea no. 269: Kindra Clineff
Idea no. 270: Toshi Otsuki
Idea no. 271: Keith Scott Morton
Idea no. 273: Ann Stratton
Idea no. 274: Brooke Slezak
Idea no. 276: Brooke Slezak
Idea no. 277: Brooke Slezak
Idea no. 278: Ann Stratton
Idea no. 279: Lisa Hubbard
Idea no. 280: Lisa Hubbard
Idea no. 281: Keith Scott Morton
Idea no. 284: Charles Gold
Idea no. 285: Andrew McCaul
Idea no. 286: Ann Stratton
Idea no. 287: Ann Stratton
Idea no. 288: Ann Stratton
Idea no. 289: Ann Stratton
Idea no. 290: Ann Stratton
Idea no. 291: Ann Stratton
Idea no. 292: Ann Stratton
Idea no. 293: Ann Stratton
Idea no. 294: Ann Stratton
Idea no. 295: Lisa Hubbard
Idea no. 296: Brooke Slezak
Idea no. 297: Lisa Hubbard
Idea no. 298: Peter Williams
Idea no. 299: Keith Scott Morton
Idea no. 300: David Prince

Index

★

221

Library of Congress Cataloging-in-Publication Data

Country living : merry & bright : 301 festive ideas for celebrating Christmas / from the editors of Country living.
    p. cm.
 Includes index.
 ISBN-13: 978-1-58816-636-4
 ISBN-10: 1-58816-636-8
1. Christmas decorations. 2. Handicraft. 3. Christmas cookery. I. Country living (New York, N.Y.)
 TT900.C4C683 2007
 745.594'12—dc22   2006038516

10 9 8 7 6 5 4 3 2 1

BOOK DESIGN BY ALEXANDRA MALDONADO

Published by Hearst Books
A Division of Sterling Publishing Co., Inc.
387 Park Avenue South, New York, NY 10016

Country Living and Hearst Books are trademarks of Hearst Communications, Inc.

www.countryliving.com

For information about custom editions, special sales, premium and corporate purchases, please contact Sterling Special Sales Department at 800-805-5489 or specialsales@sterlingpub.com.

Distributed in Canada by Sterling Publishing
C/o Canadian Manda Group, 165 Dufferin Street
Toronto, Ontario, Canada M6K 3H6

Distributed in Australia by Capricorn Link (Australia) Pty. Ltd.
P.O. Box 704, Windsor, NSW 2756 Australia

Manufactured in China

Sterling ISBN 13: 978-1-58816-636-4
      ISBN 10: 1-58816-636-8

★